Pro Tools in One Hour
(coffee break included)

Simone Corelli

Translation by
Federica Lang and Andrew Cartwright

16 March 2012

D0066981

Pro Tools in One Hour (coffee break included)
by Simone Corelli.

Translation in English by
Federica Lang and Andrew Cartwright.

Original Italian version published in 2012 by
Lambda Edizioni, Rome, Italy.

English Edition v.2

Graphic tables, cover design, and formatting by the author;
cover picture by Francesco Berardinelli.

Simone Corelli
email: simonecorelli@gmail.com
Follow us on Twitter: @PtOnehour

ISBN-13: 978-1482788532
ISBN-10: 1482788535

Contents

List of Figures

List of Tables

Foreword to the original version

"When I met Simone Corelli at a loudness workshop given in Rome, I could immediately see Simone's intelligence and audio knowledge are as eternal as the city! After I heard him speak on several audio subjects I could see his infectious enthusiasm and desire to push the envelope of audio knowledge.

His new book, "Pro Tools in un'ora", may be a little optimistic (well, maybe two hours!) but I can tell you it is a thorough (and necessary) introduction to the newest version of Pro Tools. This new version breaks several grounds and so everyone, even those familiar with previous versions, will need to be taken up to speed on the new features.

Simone is the best person I can think of to take you there, while expressively sipping your *Italian Espresso!*"

Orlando, Florida, USA, 10 December 2011
Bob Katz, Mastering Engineer, Digital Domain

Preface

Since 1999 I have been teaching students, friends, and colleagues how to use *Pro Tools*. I very soon realised that advising beginners to read the official reference manual was a losing and unsustainable battle, as that Holy Writ is a tome exceeding 1,200 pages. This largesse is surely justified in that we are talking about an impressive and complex system that is replacing technology which only 20 years ago would have occupied a whole studio—and cost a hundred times as much. In short: a guiding hand is advisable.

A typical introductory course to Pro Tools takes at least 20 hours—when you are dealing with very clever people who are familiar with using a computer and who are already involved with sound. The crazy idea of synthesizing the course in a booklet whose main chapters could be read in only 60 minutes had been seducing me for a long time and I eventually wrote it during 2011 and 2012. I published it in Italy with *Lambda Edizioni*[1].

Due to the encouragingly positive response to the original version I am now introducing the (revised) English version in electronic format, hoping that the international language and various tweaks will allow more people to derive greater satisfaction from their use of the marvellous Pro Tools.

---

[1] *Lambda Edizioni* is a small and proud publishing house that also published the comprehensive *Elementi di Cinematografia Sonora* (*Elements of Sonic Cinematography*) in 2006, written by Gilberto Martinelli, Fabio Felici, and me.

Andrew and Federica have very patiently followed my thoughts in this less than easy English translation and I warmly thank them. I also want to mention Francesco Montanari, Piero Mottola, Alberto Pinto, Sabrina Sassu, Fabio Felici, Gilberto Martinelli, Danilo Vittori, and Maurizio Armato, who tested the original version, along with Bob Katz, Yvonne Gray, Paolo Prandoni, Marco Montanari and Hidetomo Katsura for putting some finishing touches to this version.

I hope the readers will send me their opinions and suggestions to improve it further. Follow us on Twitter @PtOneHour (`http://twitter.com/PtOnehour`)!

Rome, Italy, 7 October 2012
Simone Corelli

Part I

The Essentials

CHAPTER 1

Professional Tools

Pro Tools, the renowned audio-software system that enables the digital recording, editing, and mixing of sound, was born in 1991 to the American company *Digidesign* as an evolution of *Sound Tools* (1989), which was derived from *Sound Designer* (1984). The fathers of the system are Peter Gotcher and Evan Brooks, graduates of the University of Berkeley, California.

Initially designed for *Apple Macintosh*, the system provided four-track audio and cost approximately US $6,000. It was originally divided into two parts, *ProDECK* and *ProEDIT*, which were later unified in 1993. Since those early years, success has been inevitable due to the ever-increasing interest in digital audio.

In 1995 *Digidesign* was acquired by *Avid*, manufacturer of the well-known video-editing systems, who decided to abandon its own *Audiovision* system to focus solely on the continued development of *Pro Tools* and so avoid in-house conflicts. The migration to an equivalent *Pro Tools* system was offered to *Audiovision* users.

The transition was completed in 2010 when the trademark *Digidesign* was replaced with *Avid Audio*.

1.1 Differences among the versions

Let's take a look at the macroscopic differences between the various available Pro Tools versions. Readers who are looking for more detailed information should visit Avid's Pro Tools software features web pages, where you can consult a comprehensive and comparative chart. The characteristics mentioned below will probably be more understandable once this book has been thoroughly read.

1. Pro Tools SE

   - This software is bundled with low-cost systems, in conjunction with specific two-channel interfaces by *M-Audio*, a company that was acquired a few years ago by *Avid*.

   - It allows a maximum of one master fader, fed by up to 16 mono or stereo audio tracks and eight tracks of virtual instruments that can be played back while simultaneously recording up to two tracks (two mono or one stereo) of audio. The highest sample rate is limited to 48 kHz.

   - Only included plug-ins can be used, up to a maximum of three for each track.

2. Pro Tools Express

   - Bundled with *Mbox* and *Mbox Mini* interfaces only, it allows 16 tracks, mono or stereo, 32-bit, 96 kHz files, four simultaneous audio recording tracks, eight instruments, 16 *MIDI* tracks, eight auxiliary inputs, 16 buses, one video track, *Digibase Pro* (no "Beat Detective").

3. Pro Tools MP 9

   - Only some audio interfaces by *M-Audio* can be used. It supports the control surface *C|24* and every surface that supports the *HUI protocol*.
     At the time of writing, *AAX* plug-ins aren't supported.

   - It is designed for sessions that don't use a lot of tracks: it presently manages a maximum of 48 in playback and 18 in recording, although setting the maximum sample rate at 96 kHz instead of 48 kHz reduces the amount of tracks available. It is possible to use up to 256 buses. "Beat Detective" is available but only on single track. "Beat Detective" is a tool for manipulating and editing audio material that is rhythmic in nature. You can extract a tempo map from audio and MIDI material, create a groove template, conform audio to a tempo map, conform the MIDI track tempo to an audio region.

4. Pro Tools (replaces Pro Tools LE)

- It even works with non-dedicated audio interfaces including the one already incorporated in the computer, as well as with the *MBox, Digi 002, Digi 003*, and *M-Audio* series from *Avid*. It supports *C|24, HUI*, and even *Eucon* control surfaces.

- It is ideal for editing, music production, and small-studio necessities. It is considered to be for semi-professional or, within certain limits, professional use. Hardware permitting, it can deliver up to 32-bit *floating-point* audio sampled at 192 kHz.

- It handles timecode and can import/export in the interchange formats *OMF, AAF*, and *MXF*.
  It is provided with *DigiBase Pro* to store your sound archive and is able to import tracks without any functional limitation.

- It can be expanded with *Avid*'s *Complete Production Toolkit* software, which makes it more comparable to the performance specifications of Pro Tools HD: enables mixing up to surround 7.1, supplies a maximum of 256 simultaneous audio tracks instead of 96, delivers 64 editable video tracks instead of just a non-editable one, and provides *VCA* group capability too.

5. Pro Tools HD (is dedicated to the *HD, HD Native*, and *HDX* hardware)

- It allows the use of *Avid*'s audio *HD* interfaces.
  Sound can be processed by the computer's CPU or with special-purpose cards made by *Avid* and *Universal Audio* (UAD-2), which are fitted with dedicated processors (DSP).

- Performances suitable for professional use at the highest levels are guaranteed (up to 768 audio tracks with *HDX* hardware). When combined with a prestigious control surface, such as the *D-Control* or the smaller *D-Command*, it is called the *Icon* system.

Year after year Pro Tools evolved sensibly, improving in all areas, but we cannot deny that it still suffers from certain functional problems. The extent of these problems becomes apparent when reading the documentation released with each version in the part describing the solved bugs and those that remain to be solved—how many! However, with patience and cunning, and the occasional helping hand of a friend or colleague when we find ourselves in difficulties, problems can be overcome or avoided and Pro Tools eventually gives great satisfaction.

Above all it has no real competitors as far as completeness and flexibility of the package are concerned, and when combined with the appropriate hardware it can meet the most demanding of audio requirements.

CHAPTER 2

Understanding the Mixer

The *audio mixer* is a device that enables audio signals from different sources, live or recorded, to be adjusted independently—according to the required amplitude, timbre, pan, etc.—and then combined and sent to the listening system, if necessary through a recording device so that the result can then be played by commercial audio or audiovisual devices such as CD/DVD players and mobile devices, or can be broadcast.

Mixers are usually capable of producing additional parallel independent sums (*submixes*) that can be used again as inputs.

Non-physical (software) mixers are called *virtual mixers*. From now on we will refer to the specific virtual mixer provided by Pro Tools. Let's imagine it as comprising side-by-side modules, each one a long and narrow element containing several controls. Principal among these controls is the fader, which attenuates or amplifies. We can imagine a signal being input at the top of the module and output at the bottom. Virtual cables connect our mixer modules with *inputs*, *buses*, and *outputs*.

2.1 Input, output, bus, and path

A *bus* is just a fairly simple device, on a signal route, which is capable of receiving signals from many sources, summing them, and making the result available to whatever module needs it.

It is convenient to imagine the bus as a funnel, where ingredients can be added that emerge combined.

Pro Tools provides many buses, some of them of a special kind because they are dedicated to take care of each of the physical outputs, and are accordingly called *output buses*; with the release of version 9 in 2011 the considerable number of 256 (monophonic) buses was reached, even on intermediate systems.

Please note that this book usually refers to monophonic or stereophonic (two-channel) modules, even though with higher-spec systems it is possible to work, for example, in quadraphonic or in the formats 5.1 to 7.1. However, for the purpose of understanding how Pro Tools operates, so you can derive the most out of the software, this is of little relevance since we can imagine higher-spec configurations than mono and stereo simply by combining multiple monophonic elements.

Paths   Physical inputs, buses, and physical outputs (with related output buses) are accessible only once a name, a sort of label, is assigned to them. The advantage of this name-specific assignment is that through the use of a specific table we can reassign, for example, any given input or output label to another input or output, without the need to reconfigure each module for which it is used[1].

Assigning inputs and outputs to the mixer modules is always and only done through the use of these intermediary labels. Labels are then given to the actual inputs, buses, and output buses using the assignment table mentioned above, which is accessible through the "I/O..." command (an abbreviation of input/output) from the "Setup" menu, of which you can see two example screenshots in figures 2.1, page 9 and 2.2, page 10. In Pro Tools terminology, these labels are called *paths*.

If a *path* is multichannel it is also possible to define *subpaths*, e.g. to access only the left and right front outputs, or only the one channel dedicated to the *subwoofer* in a 5.1 path.

---

[1]Since the buses, unlike the physical connections with the external world, differ only by the use we decide to make of them, it is pointless to separate the concept of label from the absolute identification of the bus. So much so that, contrary to previous versions of Pro Tools, the absolute identification number of the bus is no-longer visible and we refer to buses only through their given labels.

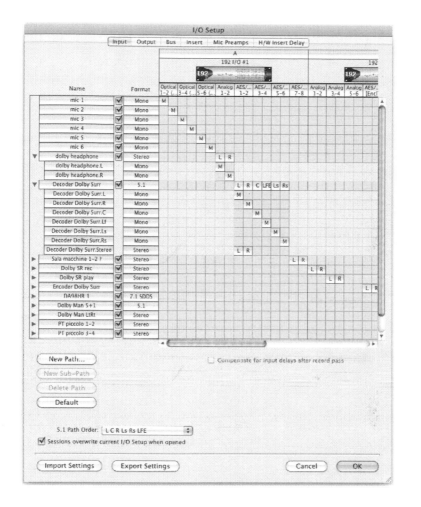

Figure 2.1: I/O configuration window showing the sub-page for creating and assigning *paths* to physical *inputs*.

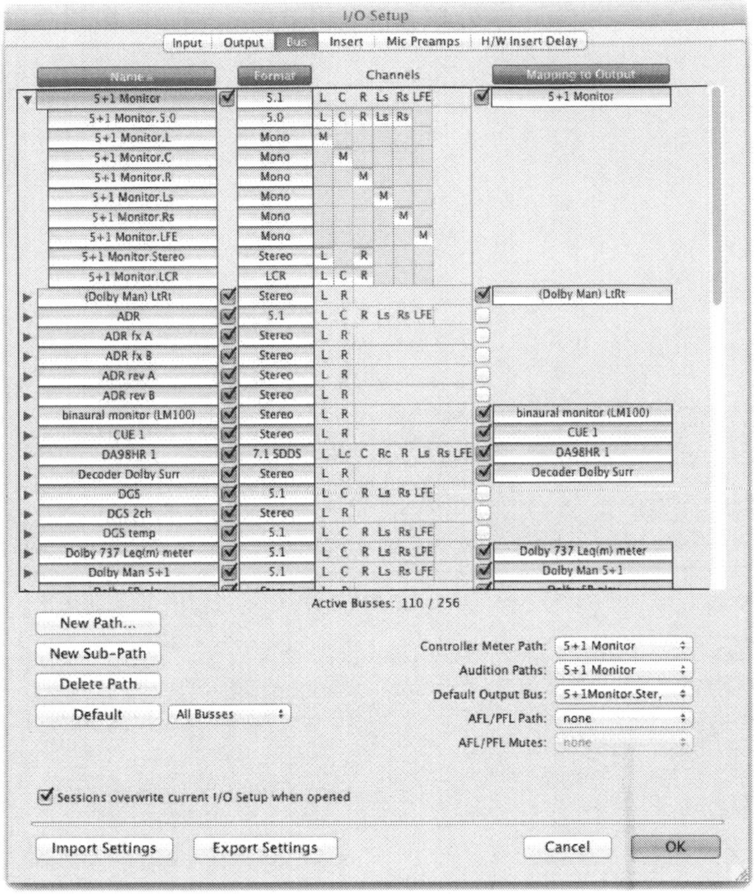

Figure 2.2: I/O configuration window for creating and assigning *paths* to (internal) *buses* and mapping (output) *buses* to physical *outputs* (see the "Mapping to Output" column). Notice the *subpaths* of the "5+1 Monitor" *path*.

✧

*It is advisable to be able to interact with a Pro Tools session as
you read. A Pro Tools document defines the mixer
configuration, the edits, the automation, and other things, and
is called a* session.
*After opening the application, create a new (blank) session
with the "New Session" command accessible in the "File" menu.
For example, set the sample rate to 48 kHz, quantisation to
24-bit, and choose BWF files format.
It is good practice to create sessions on a different storage
medium to the computer's start-up drive, which, having to
satisfy the needs of the operating system and particularly when
managing the virtual memory, is not the ideal device to
guarantee the high performances normally required by such
systems, especially with less-recent versions of Pro Tools.*

✧

2.2 Mixer modules

Let's look at the different kinds of mixer module (also known as
channel strips) in more detail.

The first module to be explained is the (stereo) *Aux Input*—the
source is stereo but the output could be mono, in which case Pro
Tools will sum the two channels. Understanding how the *Aux Input*
operates will make it easier to work with other modules.

Aux(iliary) Input

The source of the *Aux Input* can be a physical input or the output
from a bus. Notice that more than one module can be fed from the
same source without any degradation of the signal.

Once we have defined the signal source for our *Aux Input* module we can insert up to ten sound processors such as equalisers,   Inserts
compressors, limiters, and reverbs. These can be internal to the
system, in which case they are called *plug-ins*, or external, con-   Plug-ins
nected through an output and an input (in this example they will

Figure 2.3: The "Channel Strip" equaliser and dynamic processor (supplied with Pro Tools from version 10), inherited from the Euphonix mixers.

be of a stereo kind, therefore two coupled mono outputs and two coupled mono inputs), to be defined in a sub-page of the "I/O...". In practice, with the *inserts* the sound is deviated to reach one of the above mentioned virtual or real processors from where it exits, having been modified, to continue on its course inside the module through a maximum of nine more *inserts*.

In order to insert *plug-ins* or external devices it will be necessary to click on the dot to their left, on the upper part of the mixer module, which can be seen by examining figure 2.4, page 19.

After this first part the sound reaches a stage where it can be distributed to secondary destinations creating the so-called *pre-fader sends* ("pre-fader" because the signal has yet to reach and be affected by the main level regulator, known as the *main fader*). Pre-fader sends

Contrary to that which the well-plumbed metaphor of the water flow could suggest, digital sound does not lose pressure even if emissary flows are formed: they are in fact clones of the signal, which is to say absolutely perfect copies. Obviously it is not compulsory to create these additional flows, just as there's no obligation to use plug-ins or external devices (*outboard*).

An example of a typical use of these sends for secondary destinations is when we need to add artificial reverberation: the main fader manages the direct signal going to the final mix, while the send delivers the same signal to a reverb unit that generates the reverb which is fed to the final mix too. Even if it is probably premature, to gain a practical idea of this you should follow the description below of how to proceed.

1. Leaving the main fader at 0 dB, through a plug-in such as the "Trim" you set the relative level of the tracks that contain recordings of the different sound sources (e.g. musical instruments and voices), obtaining for each one a realistic level for a foreground sound. Sends: an example

2. The sends to the *bus* that will feed the reverb are set at 0 dB and in pre-fader mode[2].

---

[2]The reverberant sound field is almost constant whether the listener is closer or farther from a sound source: mainly what varies is the direct signal combined with the very first reflections, but due to the phenomenon of *masking* we get the impression that it is the reverb that is increasing or decreasing.

3. The reverb generated by a plug-in (*D-Verb*) put on an *aux input* module fed by the above mentioned *bus*, is chosen and calibrated in quality and amount.

4. In the end, for each instrument you decide the perceived distance relative to the listener by adjusting the main fader on the related mixer module, while with the *panpot*[3] you define the perceived position in space.

The creation of a secondary flow of this kind, we repeat, is called *send*, to which the specification *pre-fader* or *post-fader* is added.

Each *send* possesses a "tap", namely a small fader that determines how much of the sound is sent. It is also possible to see an instantaneous measure of signal peak and to balance the output—possibly stereo—of the send (the signal is said to be "panpotable") with two *panpots*, one for the left signal fed to the stereo output and one for the right fed to the same stereo output, or silence the whole thing with a dedicated *mute*.

After a maximum of ten sends, graphically displayed as two groups, one for the first five (A–E) and the other for the second five (F–J), the signal continues onwards and eventually reaches an instrument that indicates the signal level through two vertical bars (two because we are considering a stereophonic case). These bars contain segments with different colours, which light up depending on the peak level relative to the digital full scale (*FS* or *FSD*), according to the following scheme:

Standard level indicator

- All segments will be off when the peak levels range from complete absence of signal to -61.4 dB.

- Five green segments all light when the peak level is comprised between -61.3 dB and -54.8 dB, and other segments light up as the level approaches -12 dB.

---

[3]The panoramic potentiometer, or *panpot*, allows a signal to be distributed on more outputs, gradually passing through all the possible balances of level.
If the *panpot* is set in the centre with a stereo output, the signal will reach both mono outputs in the same way, only slightly attenuated to compensate for the double source; this attenuation (*pan depth*) in Pro Tools HD or Pro Tools with *Complete Production Toolkit* can be set between 2.5 and 6 dB, according to several factors among which are the acoustics of the listening environment and the angle subtended by the loudspeakers to the listener.

- Yellow segments from -11.9 dB to -2.9 dB.

- Orange segments over -2.8 dB.

- Two red segments in case of reaching or exceeding 0 dB.

The level indicators do not affect the sound at all, which continues towards the *main fader*—a control that, in the same way as we described for the sends, allows the signal to be amplified up to a maximum of 12 dB or attenuated down to nothing (0%, equal to $-\infty$ dB). As you will probably know, setting the fader to 0 dB (also known as 100% or *unity gain*) leaves the signal level unchanged.

The order with which the sound passes through the level indicator and the fader can be inverted: the one we just described is called *pre-fader metering*; disabling it will display a measure of the level taken after the action of the fader, namely *post-fader metering*. The command to activate one or the other behaviour is present in the "Options" menu.

At this point the sound passes to a spatialisation device, like for the sends, which in this case is represented by two *panpots*, one for each input channel; in this example, we repeat, we are treating a module with two parallel mono signals, therefore there will be two panpots on a stereo output.

In the same manner as described for the sends, here too we have a button called "Mute" that allows the signal to be interrupted, namely to silence the module as if we had completely lowered the fader, while the button named "Solo" will temporarily mute any other mixer module, letting us listen only to the one in which we are interested. However, a mixer module can be protected against this temporary silencing—caused when the solo button on another module is activated—by putting it in a state called *solo safe*, which can be engaged with a click on the "Solo" button while holding down the modifying key[4] [COMMAND].

Solo

The next step for our audio signal is to be able to be distributed to other secondary destinations, as we described when talking about

Post-fader sends

---

[4]The modifying keys are the ones that modify the effect of pressing a key, e.g. while writing, the [SHIFT] key renders the capital of the letter that is pressed.
The modifying keys on Mac computers are [SHIFT], [CTRL], [COMMAND], and [OPTION] (also called [ALT]).
For the equivalent on keyboards of Windows systems use [CTRL] instead of [COMMAND] and [START] instead of [CTRL].

the *sends*. But here only the post-fader destinations will be taken into consideration and the flow will depend also on the position of the main fader as well as on the state of the *mute*, which in this case are upstream.

Finally the stereo signal is ready to be sent to the main destination, which we can set, i.e. a bus or an output bus. The main destination can be multiple, adding parallel destinations that will receive the same signal: just press the modifying key [CTRL] when in the pop-up menu that shows the possible destinations, adding your selection to the others previously chosen. The difference with the post-fader sends lies in the fact that it will not be possible to individually regulate the level of the multiple destinations—sometimes this can be a useful restriction.

Master Fader

We spoke of the buses and thinking about them as funnels. We have to add a detail to our analogy: we have to imagine a tap at the output of each funnel; the buses are indeed provided with an output fader that is adjustable between $-\infty$ dB and $+12$ dB, which is preset to 0 dB. To modify our tap it is necessary to make it visible by revealing a particular mixer module called a *Master Fader* and then indicating to which bus or output bus the tap has to refer.

The *Master Fader* module looks like an *Aux Input* module but as we explained it is in fact used to display and allow the adjustment of each fader that already exists on every bus. The bus must be set by clicking where, in other modules, usually we see the output selection virtual button.

Moreover, it is not panpotable, you cannot generate sends, and regrettably and inexplicably there is no *mute*. It is possible, however, to include plug-in or physical inserts as we explained for the *Aux Input*, but with a fundamental and very important difference: in the *Master Fader* the inserts act *post-fader*.

Post-fader
inserts

Audio Track

The modules called *Audio Track* are identical to the *Aux Input* except that each one is assigned a recording track, which justifies the presence of a *REC* button able to arm the same track, i.e. enable it to record the set source.

Please note that, until we actually get to recording, this track will not be recording anything. Instead, when we enter the recording mode the armed *Audio Tracks* will record and the non-armed tracks will play.

Input vs Playback

In reality the matter is a bit more complex and to know what an audio track is putting out we have to know the state of the system (*stop*, *play*, or *record*) and how the audio track's monitoring of the sound is controlled by a special command found in the "Track" menu.

This command is a little counterintuitive because if "Auto Input Monitoring" is shown in the menu we are to understand that presently Pro Tools is in the inverse state known as "Input Only Monitoring", and vice versa.

The difference between the two possibilities is basically in the behaviour during playback when the track is armed: if we have chosen "Input Only Monitoring" we will always have the source as output, as with an *aux input* module, and we will not listen to what we have recorded previously[5].

We recommend setting the above option, found in the "Track" menu, to read "Input Only Monitoring" because we believe it delivers a more logical behaviour and is more suitable to a novice.

Please note that the sound you hear when recording contains a very slight delay. This is exactly how it happens on analogue tape recorders, because the playback head is situated (slightly) after the recording head.

Latency

This digital *latency* is due to several factors and can be distracting for those who are singing or playing an instrument while listening through headphones to the live output supplied by Pro Tools.

However, latency can be reduced by adjusting some parameters of the *playback engine*, which we will talk about later (5.1, page 65), or by activating, maybe only temporarily, a special mode that is accessed through the command "Low Latency Monitoring"

---

[5]On high-end Pro Tools systems you can decide what to listen to (input or playback) individually for each track acting on the button next to the *rec arm* one; there is also the possibility in the preferences of selecting between two naming schemes ("Auto Input/Input Only" (grey I, green I) vs "PEC/Direct" (green P, grey D)) and defining the behaviour when the recording is interrupted.

in the "Options" menu—which, in exchange, will impose on us some limitations. For further details we refer you to the official Pro Tools manual and especially to the manual for the specific hardware in use.

Other mixer modules

Let's proceed with the other kinds of mixer module: there is a type dedicated to the management of *MIDI* signals, called a *MIDI Track*, which handles musical performance information such as which keys are pressed and released on a musical keyboard.

There is also a hybrid MIDI+audio module called an *instrument track,* and the most powerful Pro Tools systems offer even a "mechanical" control of groups of modules through a *VCA Master* module. Such intricacies are beyond the scope of this brief guidebook.

The mixer module types are summarised, schematically, in table 2.1, page 21.

✧

To be able to face the next steps confidently it is helpful to have thoroughly absorbed all that we have covered so far. We advise a careful study of the figures 2.4, page 19 and 2.5, page 20 and perhaps a re-reading of the text—maybe after the promised coffee break.

✧

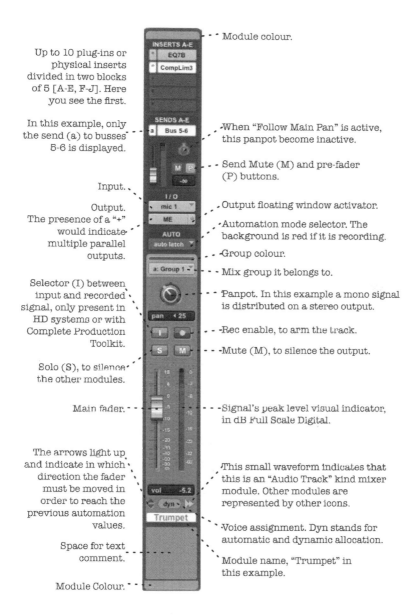

Up to 10 plug-ins or physical inserts divided in two blocks of 5 [A-E, F-J]. Here you see the first.

In this example, only the send (a) to busses 5-6 is displayed.

Input.

Output. The presence of a "+" would indicate multiple parallel outputs.

Selector (I) between input and recorded signal, only present in HD systems or with Complete Production Toolkit.

Solo (S), to silence the other modules.

Main fader.

The arrows light up and indicate in which direction the fader must be moved in order to reach the previous automation values.

Space for text comment.

Module Colour.

Module colour.

When "Follow Main Pan" is active, this panpot become inactive.

Send Mute (M) and pre-fader (P) buttons.

Output floating window activator.

Automation mode selector. The background is red if it is recording.

Group colour.

Mix group it belongs to.

Panpot. In this example a mono signal is distributed on a stereo output.

Rec enable, to arm the track.

Mute (M), to silence the output.

Signal's peak level visual indicator, in dB Full Scale Digital.

This small waveform indicates that this is an "Audio Track" kind mixer module. Other modules are represented by other icons.

Voice assignment. Dyn stands for automatic and dynamic allocation.

Module name, "Trumpet" in this example.

Figure 2.4: The mixer module for a mono audio track.

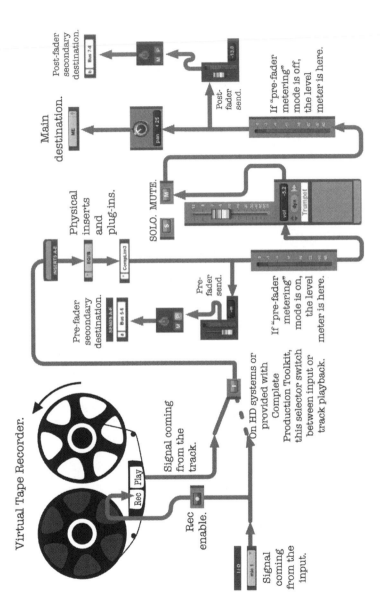

Figure 2.5: Signal flow through a mono audio track.

Mixer module	Description	Symbol
Aux Input	Receives the signal from a physical channel or from a *bus* and processes it live, supplying the result on the desired *bus* or *output bus*.	Arrow pointing downwards.
Audio Track	Similar to the above, but connected to a track on the virtual tape.	Waveform.
Master Fader	Controls the output of a *bus* or *output bus*.	Σ (sigma), the summation symbol in mathematics.
Midi Track	Records and plays back a MIDI signal.	MIDI connector (five-pin round plug).
Instrument Track	MIDI+audio hybrid.	Musical keyboard.
VCA Master	Acts on a group of modules linking, for example, their faders. It is present only on high-spec systems.	Three faders.

Table 2.1: Types of *mixer modules* we can use to make up the Pro Tools mixer. The graphic symbol that identifies the type of module is found in the lower right corner of the strip, as you can see in figure 2.4, page 19.

2.3   Automation

Now let's introduce the concept of *automation*, a term that we will often find in Pro Tools abbreviated to "auto".

There are mixing parameters that we can adjust, for example the attenuation and amplification allowed by the *faders*, the panning controlled by the *panpots*, the silencing obtainable with the main *mute* buttons as well as the ones related to the *sends*, along with the parameters of the possible *plug-ins*, all of which can have their values continuously recorded so they can be automatically recalled later on during playback, moment by moment. This is why the tracks assigned to each kind of mixer module, in addition to containing sound in the case of the *Audio Tracks* or *MIDI* commands on the *MIDI Tracks*, contain some editable lines that describe the temporal behaviour of each automated parameter.

It is possible to disable the automation function (*auto off*) as well as enable the writing (*auto write*) or reading (*auto read*) modes for each mixer module independently.

There are also mixed automation modes (*auto touch* and *auto latch*) that behave like the *read* mode until the parameter is touched. When set to *touch*, once the parameter is touched Pro Tools starts to write our changes and stops when the control is released; on the other hand, if the mode is set to *latch* instead of *touch*, the control continues to write whatever value it is set to upon its release.

Modes of automation   Recapping, the automation modes that can be activated on each mixer module are:

Write: when the system is in playback or recording (in this case excluding the armed tracks), stores the positions of the fader, panpot, and mute (including those of the sends), along with the parameters that the user has decided to automate on the plug-ins.

Read: reads previously written values or, in the absence of such written values, does nothing[6].

***

[6]The absence of an initial writing of automation values is a very dangerous trap because control settings that have never been written explicitly are freely adjustable by the user, and they will remain adjusted because the *read* mode will be unable to recall their previous values. Incidentally, the "virgin" automation is not even well highlighted on a visual level. It is therefore advisable to record an initial passage in

Touch: behaves as the read as long as no one touches the control. Once touched Pro Tools begins to write the adjustments to the control. When released it stops writing and glides back to the previously written automation value over a user-defined time, typically one or two seconds, which is set through the preferences (6.4, page 80).

Latch: behaves like the *touch* but when the control is released Pro Tools continues to write the last set value, as though the operator's fingers were frozen on the control.

Off: disables reading and writing of the automation.

We leave it for the reader to delve into the combined case of *touch+latch*, and the *trim* function that behaves differentially with respect to the previously written automation (you can alter the variations of prior automation). Note that unfortunately these two advanced functions are available only on the higher-spec Pro Tools systems.

We remind you that *faders*, *panpots*, and *mutes* (the main ones and the ones of the sends) always have automation enabled. Plug-in parameters have to be enabled expressly, by clicking on the "Auto" button at the top part of each plug-in's window or on the individual controls with the three modifiers [CTRL], [OPTION] and [COMMAND], otherwise they remain at the last set value.

We also add that the automation does not work on audio tracks enabled to record (armed) and that it's possible to make the automation follow *cut-copy-paste* actions on the timeline (see chapter 3) by enabling the "Automation Follows Edit" option, accessible from the "Options" menu.

A last note for the reader to explore at a later time: the window that appears when the command "Automation" in the "Window" menu is given allows the suspending of the automation for all tracks; see a description of this on 5.1, page 70.

2.4 Some commands

We have understood that Pro Tools provides us with a mixer complete with effects. It also provides a multitrack recorder/player for

---

write, even though very brief.

which time has come to introduce some basic keyboard commands:

- To play the system press and immediately release the [SPACE-BAR], which when pressed a second time will stop the playback.

- To record, provided of course that we have at least one armed track, use the combination [COMMAND] + [SPACE-BAR][7]; to end the recording use the [SPACEBAR], or use [COMMAND] and a full stop if you want to discard the recording.

- The [RETURN] key "rewinds the tape", or, out of metaphor, takes the cursor back to the beginning of the session.

All this will become clear as you read the next chapter, which is dedicated to editing.

---

[7]With the symbol "+" we indicate the simultaneous pressing of keys. When a combination of buttons foresees the use of modifying keys, these must be pressed before that which they modify and released immediately after that key has been released.

CHAPTER 3

How to edit

✧

To better follow this chapter we suggest that you create a few audio tracks on a new session—the command to create modules and related tracks is "New...", found in the "Track" menu.

✧

Pro Tools interfaces with us mainly through two windows: the *mix window* and the *edit window*. The *mix window* displays the mixer, which shows all of the modules we talked about in the previous chapter, laid out side by side. The *edit window* displays the behaviour of each mixer module's automated parameters in relation to the passage of time (from left to right), and even shows the recorded/edited material for audio and *MIDI* tracks.

With [COMMAND]+= (the *equals* of the small numeric keyboard proves particularly handy) you toggle from the *edit window* to the *mix window* or vice versa; if they were closed they are opened up again. Presently, closing both windows is not the same as closing the session, which can be done instead with the command "Close Session" in the "File" menu.

3.1   Clips and non-linear editing

Clips and
parent files
We introduce a fundamental definition: a *clip* (before Pro Tools 10 it was called *region*) is an index that defines a portion from a pre-existing audio (or MIDI) file called a *parent file*. Because it is simply an index pointing to something pre-existing, on its own it requires a negligible amount of memory space, i.e. the few data required to define the name and position of the parent file on the drive[1], the portion referenced inside the *parent file* (*start* and *end* positions), and a few other ancillary pieces of information.

Each clip is automatically or manually assigned a name, modifiable as desired. Also, we can define an internal point called a *sync point*, which is represented with a small triangle pointing downwards (indicated by item 11 in figure 3.1, page 30) and is very useful for synchronisation. We can also redefine the start and end of the clip relative to the parent file by extending or reducing the clip's head and tail with the provided *trim tool*, assign a colour, a quality rate up to five stars, and so on.

Clip gain
Pro Tools version 10 introduces *clip gain*, which for each clip brings the possibility of assigning a specific gain (amplification/ attenuation) that can vary throughout the duration of the clip. The result will of course be combined with the gain set with the mixer's faders on the audio track to which the clip pertains. To use this new function it is helpful to make the gain of the clip visible with the "Clip Gain Line" command in the "Clip" submenu of the "View" menu. An example is clearly visible on the second track in the just mentioned figure.

A file can be parent to many clips, some of which may overlap one another. For example, the case could be that while recording Vivaldi's *Four Seasons* one clip will be defined for the whole concert, one for each season, and others for the various movements that each season comprises. Clearly, the maximum size of the clip cannot be larger than the size of the parent file.

---

[1]*Device, drive,* and *volume* are terms that express slightly different concepts even though in practice they are used as synonyms: the storage *device* can be of different types, for example the *Solid State Devices* have been introduced recently, in which there are no moving parts, while with the term *drive* we should refer to the ones with spinning discs. *Volume* indicates an amount of memory provided with a single *file system*, which could physically reside on a partition of a drive or other device.

Also, each clip can be used more than once within the track we are editing, as well as on different tracks, even simultaneously.

As a matter of fact, when we move audio or *MIDI* clips, Pro Tools is not really moving any material in the storage device: the editing is virtual and it is only during playback that the devices that contain the files read and supply the needed information moment by moment, allowing you to enjoy the sound of your arranged sequence.

Non-Linear Editing

The combination of random access and non-destructive editing is called *non-linear editing*. This has become so commonplace due to the power and speed of computers and drives that it is considered the rule by now and no one even notices it anymore.

At the end of our recording, editing, mixing, and mastering work, when we want to share the result with others who might not own Pro Tools, we will generate one simple audio file where the result is "printed". We will obtain this through the buses and a final track that will receive and record the signal, or via the inadvisable "Bounce to" command situated in the "File" menu.

3.2 Exploring the edit window

Taking advantage of the open session on the computer, and continuing to refer to fig. 3.1, page 30, let's get acquainted with the *edit window*.

On the horizontal axis we have the *timeline* while on the vertical axis we see that which corresponds to each mixer module, which is to say tracks arranged in the same order as the mixer modules are arranged in the *mix window* (though tracks here are arranged from top to bottom instead of from left to right).

Timeline

It is also possible to import a *video track* (video tracks do not have a counterpart in the mixer!) that the most powerful versions of Pro Tools allow you to edit, as seen in chapter 4, page 5.

Each mixer module and related track in the edit window can be hidden from view or made visible again (*hide* and *show*) by clicking on the dot to the left of their name in the *Track List* overview column called *TRACKS*, found at the top left of both the edit and mix windows. To show or hide the area containing the TRACKS column you need to click on the small button found on the window border at the far bottom left, indicated by item 02.

Show/Hide

It should be noted that below the above mentioned track list column we also have a box for the *GROUPS* list. In fact we can gather (the technical term is *group*) several tracks and/or the related modules on the mixer, which enables the editing of multiple tracks in parallel and/or the linking of faders and other parameters of the mixer modules.

It is possible to individually enable or disable each of these mix and edit groups, although a default group exists that cannot be deleted, called *<All>*, with which you tie all visible tracks and/or all the related modules (alternatively, material on all visible tracks can even be easily selected by dragging in the *timebase ruler*).

The control of edit and mix groups can, as per preferences, be unlinked, allowing the independent enabling or disabling of the edit or mix bond in a group that has both kinds.

✧

How do you select multiple items? To select all items from the first to the last in a sequence and including extremes, just select one of the two extremes by clicking on it, then do the same to the other extreme while holding the [SHIFT] key. When instead you want to add or remove an item from those presently selected, just click on the item while holding the [COMMAND] key. Try this out on the names of the tracks (item 05 in the figure) by selecting and deselecting some of them.

✧

To create a *group* you select two or more mixer modules, or equivalently the corresponding tracks in the edit window, and press [COMMAND]+G (or use the command present in the "Track" menu). You can now specify a name, a letter of the alphabet, the type (*mix group*, *edit group* or both), and the functions to be linked together[2] (such as *mute* and *solo*).

---

[2]On Pro Tools HD or Pro Tools with *Complete Production Toolkit* option the possibilities are much more numerous, such as allowing the parameters of plug-ins to be linked as well.

For example, try and create a group with tracks 1, 2, and 5. Once created, disable it and re-enable it by clicking on the group name, which is visible in the little special-purpose column at the bottom left of the edit window, or by typing the letter of the alphabet previously associated with it if the *a..z* group button is active.

Let's have a look at some other interesting points highlighted in fig. 3.1, page 30:

03: Click and hold, and a list appears of possible *timebase rulers* that can be enabled and disabled, which express time in minutes and seconds or in *samples* or in musical units, as we will see on 3.4, page 34. Once they are visible you can choose the unit of measurement for the time counters; an alternative is to use the pop up menu that can be enabled clicking on the small triangle on the right of the main counter.

06: By clicking and holding on this vertical ruler it is possible to choose how much vertical space to allow for the visualisation of the track.

08: It's a button that activates the "Link Timeline and Edit Selection" mode. It is strongly advised to keep this switched on (highlighted in light blue), at least for now. We will mention this in 5.1, page 64.

09: Prevents the cursor from returning to the starting point after a playback, therefore there may be cases in which it will be useful to disable it but generally, for now, we advise to keep it switched on.

15: Shows or hides the small display of the whole session, called *universe view* where you can click to rapidly reach any point in the session. We advise you give it a try.

3.3   Editing modes and tools

Before working with the *edit window* it is important first to learn about the tools you can use for audio and *MIDI* material, and on automation lanes.

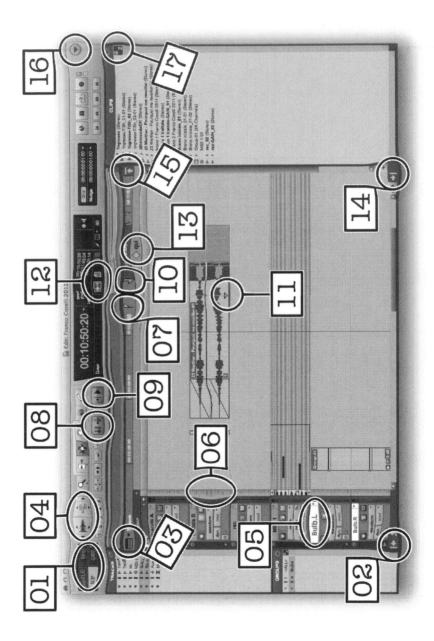

Figure 3.1: The *edit window*. The numbered (and magnified) items are commented on in the text.

Let's turn our eyes to the area that is in the top part of the *edit window*. From the left (item 01 in the figure) we see the four alternative editing modes as described below.

Shuffle: in which additions or deletions of material on the timeline cause the subsequent clips to move correspondingly.

Slip: a bond-free mode, in which the editing operations do not interfere with the material placed before or after.

Spot: seldom used, it requires the numerical setting of the head, tail, or *sync point* positions of the clips dragged onto the timeline or touched with the grabber tool that we will describe in a short while.

Grid: similar to the *slip*, except it snaps the cursor positioning on the *timeline* to a grid value (of absolute or relative kind) that can be set by the user, and can be revealed or hidden by clicking on the word "grid" at the top right of the *edit window*.

We advise that you avoid the dangerous *shuffle* and use, initially, the simple and intuitive *slip* mode. For security, when you apply [COMMAND]+click on the *shuffle* button, a thoughtfully provided protection lock will appear which indicates that *shuffle* cannot be enabled.

Proceeding to the right, a cluster of rectangular buttons (item 04) provide control for the *zoom*. Try it now by clicking and holding on one of the two arrows pointing left or right and drag, so obtaining a continuous horizontal zoom, which is to say on the time axis. This can also be obtained with particular combinations of keys and wheels depending on the pointing device used (on Apple's *Magic Trackpad* you have to drag two fingers vertically while holding [OPTION]).

Immediately to the right we have the tools, from the magnifying lens to the small pencil. Use of the lens, or *zoomer*, is entirely intuitive except for the fact that you obtain the inverse operation adding the modifier key [OPTION].

Zoomer

The next tool is called the *trim*, which when selected allows you to redefine the head and tail of the clips by dragging them horizontally. When editing the automation instead, the *trim* tool

Trim

allows for the vertical movement of the *automation breakpoints* included in the selection.

Selector   The following tool, represented by an audio waveform with a colour inversion shown in the middle, is called *selector*. The *selector* is used to position the cursors defining the selection on the *timeline*, if necessary over several tracks: click and holding will set one of the two ends of the wanted selection, while dragging will set the other end. The position of these two points, called *start* and *end*, is represented on the timebase ruler respectively by an arrow pointing downwards (item 10 in the figure) and one pointing upwards, and will show as blue, or red if at least one track is armed.

The usefulness of selecting an area of edited material is easily understood. For example, once a selection is defined, pressing the [DELETE] key will erase the selected material.

Note that a single click, without holding, simultaneously positions the *start* and *end* cursors at the same point, perfectly coinciding. This is highlighted by the blinking of the cursor and the duration of the selection showing zero, as can be verified further along on the right, in the counters section.

Double clicking selects the entire underlying *clip*.

An alternative way of making a selection of material is to position the two cursors at one end then, while holding the [SHIFT] key to keep one cursor in place, set the other end with the usual click.

Using the   To position the cursor with precise accuracy at one end of the
Tabulator   clip, place it slightly to the left with a click then press the [TAB] key, which will move the cursor on to the next cut, be it the start or end of a clip or of a *fade*[3], or a *sync point*. The possibility of locking the position of one of the cursors by holding the [SHIFT] key and moving the other one is valid here as well. It will also be useful to know that if you add the modifier [OPTION] to the [TAB] key you will get a jump to the previous cut instead of to the next one.

Grabber   The *grabber* tool, identified by a small hand, allows you to pick up the clips positioned on the tracks (or on the *clip list*, which we will see afterwards, where it is possible to pick up clips independently on the selected tool) and move them from track to track (vertical move) and in time (horizontal move).

---

[3]We will meet the *fades* better on 4.1, page 42.

Click and hold the *grabber* tool on the small black triangle underneath and it will be possible to choose similar but alternative grabber-type tools from a pop-up menu.

The *grabber* tool can even be used to create or move *breakpoints* when editing the automation lanes.

The button with the speaker icon identifies the *scrubber* tool, Scrubber with which you can move the playback head directly along the virtual tape, making it accurately follow your hand movement or controlling its speed (a function called *shuttle*) by adding the modifier key [OPTION]. In truth you can easily work without this tool, since playback at half-speed is always possible with [SHIFT] + [SPACE-BAR] and, by taking advantage of the high-quality representation of the waveforms, with experience you will become accustomed to distinguishing at a glance the single letters pronounced by a voice. Additionally, holding [CTRL] when using the *selector* will temporarily transform it into the *scrubber*.

Finally: the *pencil* is used for notes and *MIDI* events or to lit- Pencil erally draw the audio waveform (when *zoom* is at its maximum). We caution against this last usage if not performed upon a physical duplication[4] of the clip, which creates a new file and thereby ensures you can recover the original file in case of an error.

If, while clicking and holding on the word *waveform* that is situated a little below the name of each audio track, we choose between the automation lanes proposed by the menu that pops-up, for example the volume[5] or *pan* lanes, this tool will allow you to draw the automation itself, by freehand or with other very imaginative methods that are accessible by clicking and holding on the *scrubber* tool button.

Once you are familiar with the above mentioned tools, we might explore a three-in-one combination called the *smart tool*, which can Smart Tool be enabled by clicking on the frame around the *trim*, *selector*, and *grabber* tools, and disabled by clicking on any of the available tools. According to the position of the cursor in relation to the clip (lower half, upper half, ends, a corner) Pro Tools will magically activate the appropriate tool.

---

[4]The "Duplicate" command uses the same clip. It does not create a new file. If needed, the command "Consolidate" can be used, as described on 5.1, page 54.

[5]More properly called *gain* or *volume control*, as *volume* is a final effect that is perceptual and dependent upon the original signal.

3.4   Other elements

Time scales   By clicking on the small triangle of the main counter it is possible to choose the time units, choosing among the following:

Bars/Beats for musical purposes.

Min:Secs i.e. minutes and seconds, with a further subdivision into milliseconds.

Time Code expressed in *hh:mm:ss:ff*, i.e. hours, minutes, seconds and frames. In some cases Pro Tools shows two more digits indicating subframes; a subframe is 1/100th of a frame.

Feet+Frames which are old-school cinematographic[6] units.

Samples i.e. number of *samples* from the beginning of the *timeline*, with the first sample identified as zero, the second as one, and so on.

"Samples" is in fact the internal format with which Pro Tools really operates and from which all other possible measures are calculated (in the *Time Code* case, once Pro Tools adds an offset that can be defined inside the window that pops up after giving the command "Session Start", and in the cinematographic case taking into account the "Current Feet+Frames Position. . . "; both present in the "Setup" menu[7]).

It will be useful to know that by clicking on the time counters, or pressing the asterisk on the *numeric keypad*, it is possible to indicate a position by entering its value numerically.

It is important to verify the state of the two icons (item 12) set below the counters because with their colour, green or red, they Relink   indicate whether Pro Tools has been able to recover and reconnect (*relink*) all the necessary files, and therefore whether the session on which we are working is whole. When a session is opened and

---

[6]The 35mm film uses 16 frames per foot of length. When using the measure Feet+Frames the frames are counted from 0 to 15 before going back to zero having increased the feet counter by one unit. The screening speed is 24 frames per second, therefore a 100-minute film measures up to almost two miles.

[7]The succession of the various versions of Pro Tools has sometimes led to the renaming or moving of some commands: "Session" was called "Session Setup" and used to reside in the "Window" menu.

some clips are not relinked to the parent file, Pro Tools will ask how to behave. To be more accurate, the icon on the left refers to files that have been used in the editing, while the one on the right is related to all the indicated clips present in the *clip list*, which is a sort of container from which clips can be dragged to the tracks. The *clip list* is visible in the right column, which if hidden can be revealed by clicking on the small button to the bottom right end of our edit window (item 14). Note that clips that coincide with the whole of their parent file are highlighted in bold. Clip list

Over the *clip list* there is the title *CLIPS*, to the right of which a small button (item 16) allows access to the rich and precious pop-up menu that we will look at in 5.1, page 71. The most important command in this menu is probably the "Export Clips as Files...", with which you can export, for example, the final recording of a mix in a 44.1 kHz, 16 bit interleaved stereo format to make an Audio-CD.

In versions previous to 10, Pro Tools used monophonic files only, paired in twos for stereo use and in groups of up to eight for the format 7.1[8], so when importing an *interleaved audio file* it had to separate the channels and so generate more mono files. These files would typically be placed in the *Audio Files* folder of the session in use, even though inside the *clip list* the related clips would be visually compacted, allowing them to be dealt with as one multichannel—a clickable small triangle would highlight their monophonic nature and allow them to be used individually.

The *session* (that's the document created with Pro Tools) is stored on disc along with the *Audio Files* folder that is usually the default destination for the imported, recorded, and/or generated audio files. In Pro Tools versions prior to 10 there is also a *Fade Files* folder that contains—rendered in advance for performance reasons that rapidly became obsolete—*fade-ins*, *fade-outs*, and *crossfades*. Session Files

There are also folders for the video files and for the automatic backups, for the plug-in settings that are exclusively dedicated to the specific session, and the file *WaveCache.wfm* that allows a fast display of the waveforms at various levels of enlargement[9].

---

[8]As we have explained already, you can only go beyond two-track stereophony with the HD systems or buying the *Complete Production Toolkit* option.

[9]The mechanism, which has a significantly positive impact on usability, is very similar to that of the *bitmap fonts* that speed up the drawing of *vector fonts*. Pay at-

There is also a folder with the definition of any exported *Clip Groups* (we will talk about this on 5.1, page 58; we say in advance that they are *playlist* portions), which is needed to make them available to other sessions through the "Export Clip Groups" found in the *clip list*'s pop-up menu.

tention though to what happens with 32 bit floating-point audio files: the graphic of the waveform (so far) is not able to correctly visualise levels above 0 dB FS, showing a false clipping.

CHAPTER 4

Action!

Now that you know some of the theory behind Pro Tools you can move on to the practice. Using the command "Playback Engine..." in the "Setup" menu, select the audio interface dedicated to Pro Tools or the set of generic interfaces, including the one built-in to the computer, in this case choosing "Pro Tools Aggregate I/O" and verifying its configuration through the appropriate means for the operating system[1], which can be accessed from the command "MIDI Studio...", found in the "MIDI" submenu of the "Setup" menu.

Having opened a new and blank *session*, create a stereo *audio track* with the command "New..." in the "Track" menu. The options that will appear are easy to follow except (probably) for the last item, which allows the choice between "Samples" or "Ticks"; for now choose "Samples", the other possibility being dedicated to a flexible musical timeline that is susceptible to metronomic time changes, which is a case that lies outside our introductory purposes.

Once the track is created we will be able to rename it at will with a double click on its name on the track (item 05 in figure 3.1, page 30) or on the corresponding *mixer module*, where you have to set a suitable output destination by indicating a *path* that will allow you to hear our exercise.

Verify the setting of the "I/O..." in the "Setup" menu and the related connection to the listening system, made up of amplifiers and loudspeakers or headphones (usually the audio interfaces duplicate

---

[1]On Macs you have to launch the "Audio MIDI Setup" application.

Figure 4.1: An *AudioSuite* plug-in, in this example the AAX "Signal Generator".

outputs 1 and 2 on the headphones output). Refer to figure 2.2, page 10 as an example.

By clicking on the small triangle at the right of the main counter on the *edit window*, select *Min:Secs* as the main timescale.

Select a few seconds of empty space on the audio track by dragging (as already explained) or by clicking on two of the three counters (*Start*, *End* and *Length*) and entering your choice numerically[2]—the third counter automatically sets itself accordingly. Then go to the "AudioSuite" menu, choose the "Other" submenu and select the "Signal Generator".

AudioSuite effects   The "AudioSuite" menu is used to manipulate the sound in different ways by acting on the audio files, not on the mixer's real-time signal flow. *AudioSuite* effects are, in short, the equivalent of the plug-ins that we insert on the mixer modules, though Pro Tools quickly "renders" results on file, either by creating a new file or by overwriting the existing one, if we so prefer (we'll come to this in a while).

Going back to the command "Signal Generator", a floating window (figure 4.1, page 38) will now have opened through which

[2]It is useful to know that by typing a "+" or a "-" before the numbers you can task the system to calculate the sum or the difference related to the previous value

we will be able to set some parameters. The contents of the upper and lower sections of this window are common for almost all of the effects and understanding them is fundamental to learning how *AudioSuite* operates.

The rectangular button in the upper top left indicates the type of *AudioSuite* effect chosen; just below this we can choose whether to act irreversibly by overwriting the parent file ("overwrite" mode) or to create a new file for each clip included in the selection ("create individual files"), or even to generate a single continuous file for every selected track ("create continuous file"). Choose the latter method for this practical example.

To the right and up a bit we have the possibility of choosing between "playlist" and "clip list", indicating on which material Pro Tools is to act, namely on the selected clips on the tracks or on the selected clips in the *clip list* (there is also a preference that links the two selections or keeps them independent). In our case this has no meaning because the "Signal Generator" creates from nothing; it does not modify any existing material.

It is important to verify if the option immediately to the right, i.e. "USE IN PLAYLIST", is highlighted in blue and therefore active: this determines whether the result of the processing will substitute the original on the edited tracks or if it will simply be added to the *clip list* for possible future use.

What is a *playlist*? It is a sequence of clips (including *fade-ins,* Playlist *fade-outs,* and/or *crossfades*), along with any gaps among them that would be played back as silence, and can be placed on one single track for possible playback by the system.

It will now be easy to understand an *alternate playlist*[3]. Access to alternative *playlists* and their management happens through a menu that appears by clicking on the small triangle to the right of the name of each track. If the vertical size of the track is too small, you can click on the grey vertical ruler on the right of the level indicator of each track in the *edit window* (item 06 of figure 3.1, page 30) to set other vertical dimensions; generally "medium" is the right compromise to clearly see the clips and have a good deal of tracks shown on the monitor at the same time..

---

[3]Unfortunately Pro Tools does not currently tie the automation to the *playlist*. Instead the automation is tied to the track, and so the possibility of managing *alternate playlists* loses lots of potential.

Below the two buttons we mentioned, there is another one that lets you choose between "entire selection" or "clip by clip": in this last case Pro Tools behaves as though we were giving the command to each selected clip individually, which in truth influences the result only for some particular effects such as "Normalize".

Another important button, still in the left area of each track in the edit window, is the one where you can choose between *waveforms*, *automation* lines of various nature, and two or three more options that we will leave out for now. The meanings are intuitive but we advise that you experiment a little to become familiar with their use.

Let's set the parameters by opting for "create continuous file" and "playlist", activating "USE IN PLAYLIST", setting the frequency to 1,000 Hz and the level to -20.0 dB, choosing "Sine" signal, and selecting "peak" measurement instead of "rms".

A click on "Render" causes Pro Tools to generate a new file and place this "daughter" clip on the timeline according to the position of the *start* and *end* cursors. By pressing the [SPACEBAR] we will be able to put the system in playback mode and so listen to the result. With the same key you can stop the playback.

To the left of the "Render" button there is a modifiable value, expressed in seconds, that indicates to Pro Tools whether to apply the effect (or to generate the file from scratch in cases such as the "signal generator") on the parent file extending a little over the start and end of the selection (this function is available from version 10 Handles onwards). Obtaining a result that you can "open" at the head and tail (known as a clip that provides *handles*) is fundamental, for example, to the ability to apply *crossfades*: imagine you want to apply a two-second crossfade to two contiguous clips; the clip on the left must have material in the parent file that continues to at least one second after the present end of the clip, while symmetrically the clip on the right will need to have material stored from a minimum of one second before its present head (see fig. 4.2, page 41).

Going back to our exercise, note that by choosing the *grabber* tool, which is to say the small hand, we can name the clips as we like with a double click, while with a *drag and drop* we will be able to move them to the left, right or even vertically to another track provided there is another one of the same type (in this example a stereo *audio track* or equally two mono audio tracks placed next

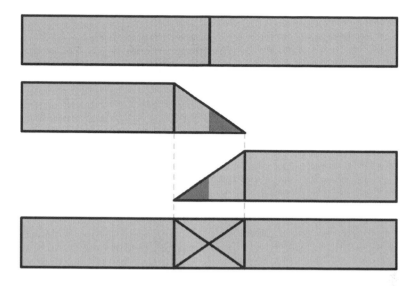

Figure 4.2: To apply a crossfade you need additional stuff.

to each other). While holding the modifying key [OPTION] you can drag and drop to duplicate the material, i.e. the original stays where it is and you will move a copy, as in *copy and paste*.

Duplicate while dragging

4.1 Synchronising

We now wish to introduce the clip synchronisation and it would be useful to create another stereo *audio track*. This time let's create one by using the related keyboard shortcut [COMMAND] +[SHIFT]+N.

Using the *selector* tool, position the (double) cursor with a click on the first or second track in a spot that is away from the clip. To move the clip to align its head to the cursor position, choose the *grabber* again and click on the clip while holding the [CTRL] key; to move the tail to align with the cursor, click while holding the [CTRL] and the [COMMAND] keys.

A very useful side effect to aligning the cursor with the head of a clip is that you can now move said clip from one track to the other with the absolute guarantee that it will not move horizontally. To do so just select the clip: the start cursor will move to its beginning and you can now drag and drop while holding the modifying [CTRL] key. This will snap the clip horizontally to where the start cursor is positioned, which in this case will be exactly where the clip is placed already, in effect constraining the clip and so allowing only vertical movement, i.e. from track to track.

Sync Point   Were we to define any point inside the clip as a *sync point* (as already mentioned in the previous chapter and indicated with number 11 in the figure 3.1, page 30) we could have Pro Tools move the clip so that its internal sync point ends up exactly where we want it to be. To define the *sync point* just position Pro Tool's time cursor where desired inside the clip and use the combination keys [COMMAND]+<comma>. Do it now.

Let's try what we just described by moving the time cursor to a random point away from the clip and then giving the usual click with the grabber on the clip, this time holding the [CTRL] key and the [SHIFT] key.

Fade   To create a *fade-in* (or a *fade-out*) make a selection that includes the head (or tail) of a clip, then press [COMMAND]+F to obtain a *fade* whose duration is precisely limited to the overlap of your selection and the clip. A window will appear (fig. 4.3, page 43) in which you can set the related *fade* parameters; you will see in the preferences that it is possible to program the kind of *fade* to your liking, so that we can avoid opening this window simply by entering [COMMAND]+[CTRL]+F to use your default *fade* settings if appropriate. If the selection concerns two neighbouring clips then a *crossfade* will be generated, provided that there is enough audio material to lengthen the tail of the clip on the left and the head of the clip on the right sufficiently to cover the shared part where we want to create the *crossfade* as seen in fig. 4.2; if there's insufficient audio material Pro Tools will highlight the problem and propose the necessary shortening of the *crossfade*.

Virtual cut   To cut a clip into two parts you place the (double) cursor in the required position then press [COMMAND]+E. The new clips so created will be automatically named, inheriting the name of the original clip with an incremental number appended to it.

It is also possible to create three clips at once, by selecting a portion from within the mother clip and pressing the above mentioned [COMMAND]+E once. The two virtual cuts that will generate the

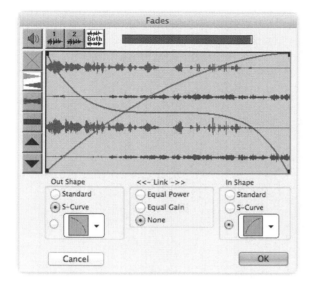

Figure 4.3: The (not so elegant) fades dialogue allows you to select the envelope shape choosing among "Standard", "S-Curve" and seven more presets.

three new clips will occur, as it is easy to guess, at the ends of the selection.

Now create a *group* by clicking on the name of one track to select it and using [COMMAND]+click to select another track, and then finally pressing [COMMAND]+G, which will make a window[4] appear where we can indicate the kind of group ("Edit", "Mix", or both; choose this last possibility) and other parameters including the name of the group and an identifying letter of the alphabet that is useful to quickly enable/disable the same.

You will have noticed a small square with the letters "a" and "z", which in the *edit window* is offered three times: top right at the

Practicing groups

a..z

---

[4]As we mentioned already, extra functions are present in the more powerful Pro Tools systems: for example you can link the controls of plug-ins belonging to different mixer modules.

end of the timebase ruler, to the right of the word "GROUP", and
finally to the right of the word "CLIPS" (item 17 in figure 3.1,
page 30). Only one of these three can be highlighted at a time, and
thereby enabled, and this choice defines the effect of pressing the
alphabetical keys on the keyboard, choosing respectively among:

- *focus mode*, i.e. a risky quick mode in which it is not necessary
  to press the [COMMAND] key to obtain a command,

- enabling or disabling of individual *groups* (each *group*, as has
  been said, is associated to a different letter of the alphabet for
  this very purpose),

- selecting in the *clip list* the first clip whose name begins with
  that letter..

Once the *group* has been created let's edit the two tracks in
parallel, by adjusting only one of them. Then try moving one of the
two faders in the mix window or on your *control surface* and note
how the other moves accordingly. You can hold down [CTRL] to
temporarily ungroup the mixer.

It is also possible to disable the "group" by clicking on the
group name in the dedicated column at the bottom left of the
mix window (if hidden, press the small button at the corner in
the bottom left, shown in the figure 3.1 as item 02), while with
[COMMAND]+[SHIFT]+G you enable or disable all groups simultaneously.

Nudging   Let's see now how to move a clip in predefined steps on the
timeline. Just select the clip with the *grabber*, or with a double click
using the *selector*[5], then press either the "-" (minus) or "+" (plus)
key on the numeric keypad: the clip will shift a step backward or
forward by an amount that is equal to the *Nudge* value that is set in
the specific little square icon at the top right of the edit window[6].

---

[5]Considering this manoeuvre, and adding that by pressing [CTRL] the *selector*
transforms temporarly into a *scrubber*, you will realise that you can use the *selector*
for almost every task.

[6]With a *right click* of the mouse in the top area of the *edit window* it is possible to
decide the availability of some buttons and indicators. In this book, "click" signifies
the pressing of the primary (usually "left") mouse or pointer button, whereas "right
click" signifies pressing the secondary button.

Extremely useful!

Sooner or later it will be necessary to store a position on the   Memory
timeline. This can be done by pressing the [RETURN] key on the   Locations
numeric keypad (some keyboards don't have one, substituting a
combination of keys instead) to create a *memory location* (shown as
a little yellow marker with a vertical line, item 13 in the figure 3.1,
page 30).

Memory locations are useful for memorising and recalling the
position of the *start* cursor (*marker*) or a selection's *start* and *end*
cursors (*selection*), as well as some other very useful features such
as the *show/hide* status and the vertical dimensions of all the tracks.
It's a good idea to have the *marker ruler* displayed among the rulers
on the timeline; to do this you should explore the "View" menu or
use item 03 as indicated in the figure of the *Edit Window*, and so
cause the dedicated menu to appear.

Holding the modifying key [COMMAND] while pressing the
"5" on the numeric keypad will cause a floating window appear
with the list of the *memory locations*; try to recall them (click on
the desired one), delete them ([OPTION]+click), and modify their
settings ([CTRL]+click).

The *memory locations* can be recalled also by quickly typing their
(possibly multi digit) identification number followed by <period>,
all of which must be done on the numeric keypad providing that the
"classic" mode is set in the preferences, on the sub–page "Operations".

To delete a *marker* just drag its icon down and release, as we
are accustomed to doing with *tabs* in word processors.

✧

*We advise practising a little to ensure you fully grasp these
pieces of information before going on to the next section, which
brings the first part to a close with an exercise on the mixer.*

✧

4.2   An exercise in setting up the mixer

Let's imagine that we have to mix the audio comment to a video that shows a picture sequence. We foresee a narration and incidental music, with a possibility of crossfading the tail of one music clip with Video   the head of the next. Importing the video is done by a dedicated command in the "File" menu.

Let's configure the mixer described in table 4.1, page 47, where the plug-ins are indicated with square brackets and the sends in round brackets, while *none, out bus,* and *bus* indicate the type of *path.*

While you do this exercise, which also requires you to access the "I/O..." to configure outputs and needed *buses*, ensure that the recording track of the final mix is armed, and that the system plays back the input of such a track ("Input Only Monitoring" mode activated, see 2.2, page 17).

Once the mix is ready, and having taken good advantage of the automation that can record your every adjustment on the mixer, it will be possible to record the result on the dedicated "Rec mix" track, and then export the new stereo clip in a useful media-format that can be integrated with your preferred video-editing software. Do take the time to verify that what has been created works properly, referring to figure 4.4, page 48.

It will also be very instructive to analyse the structure of the numerous *template sessions* that Pro Tools provides in the window that pops up when you give the command "New Session..." and choose "Create session from Template...".

Input path	Module name	Module type, [plug-in], (send)	Output path
-	Video	Video track	-
none	Narration	Mono audio track [eq. + reverb]	bus: mix
none	Mus A	Stereo audio track [eq.] (bus: revmus)	bus: mix
none	Mus B	Stereo audio track [eq.] (bus: revmus)	bus: mix
bus: revmus	Music reverb	Stereo aux input [reverb]	bus: mix
bus: mix	Rec mix	Stereo audio track	out bus: speakers + headphones
-	Speakers master	Stereo master fader [time adjuster]	out bus: speakers
-	Phones master	Stereo master fader [time adjuster + hipass filter]	out bus: headphones

Table 4.1: Configuration of the mixer proposed in the exercise.

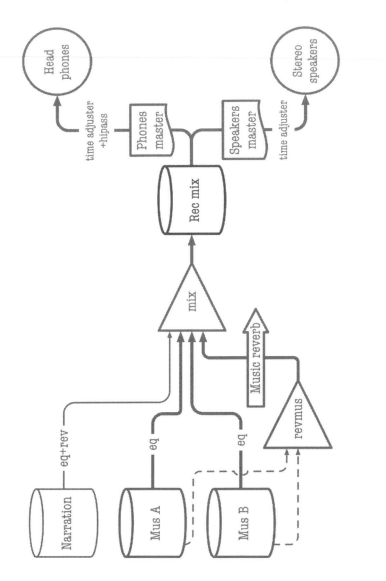

Figure 4.4: Graph related to the configuration of a minimal mixer following the example in table 4.1. With triangles we indicate the buses, with circles the outputs, with the arrow-shaped container an aux input, with the "flag" polygons the master faders.

✧

*The caffeine-fuelled hour to which we had committed ourselves
to introduce the reader to the essential basics of Pro Tools is
probably thoroughly spent.*
*Now that we can stand on the foundation laid in this first part,
with the second part we will nose through the menus to
significantly improve your familiarity with the system. We will
reveal the most important commands and the dozens of
preferences that it is often better to know even if only to get out
of trouble. A selection of the most useful keyboard shortcuts
will follow, which we strongly advise you to learn by heart.*

✧

Part II

In-Depth Examination

CHAPTER 5

Exploring the Commands

In this chapter we describe many of the commands that are available on the menu bar or in the pop-up menus, leaving out those with intuitive meanings and lingering little or not at all on those that are rarely used and not essential, unless they represent a good excuse to introduce wider concepts.

5.1 Menu bar

"File" **menu** contains many typical commands related to the opening, saving, and closing of sessions. To quit the program use "Quit Pro Tools", which is the last command in the menu immediately to the left of this one.

Let's see two particularly interesting commands:

"Save Copy In..." is useful when you want to generate a copy of the session with all the necessary files gathered (duplicated, leaving the originals untouched) in one folder.

Note that if the present session points at, for example, audio files that are in different folders then it is possible that there could be some with the same name; to prevent Pro Tools from automatically renaming these by adding a number (starting from 1), select the *Preserve Folder*

Hierarchy option that reproduces the original structure of folders and subfolders[1].

"Import" Unfortunately with Pro Tools you can open only one session at a time, precluding the possibility of a classic *cut and paste* from one session to the other. Nevertheless, this command allows you to import entire tracks from other sessions, including those in the interchange *AAF* and *OMF* formats, and to import simple audio, video, and *MIDI* files into the session. All of this can be done by *drag and drop* too.

Concerning importing tracks from other sessions we have to highlight at least two characteristics: in the "Audio Media Options", choosing "Copy from Source Media" when importing triggers the generation of a local copy of the audio files from the track's parent folder to the *Audio Files* folder of the current session, while by choosing "Link to Source Media" Pro Tools will refer to the originals; among the "Main Playlists Options" it is important to note the options "Replace" and "Overlay", useful in case one or more tracks are imported over others that already exist, rather than as new tracks[2].

"Edit" **menu** is an important menu containing commands related to editing that affect the current selection or part of it:

"Heal Separation" replaces virtual cuts if the clip on the left and the one on the right belong to the same parent file and are virtually contiguous.

"Consolidate" creates a new file containing an image of a track's accumulated events in the selection (including all selected clips, gaps, fades, and crossfades, applying *clip gains* but excluding any underlying track's automation). For example, had we created a sequence by arranging various clips generated with the "Signal Generator" *AudioSuite* plug-in, we could select the sequence and, by

---

[1]This helps PT to *relink* the files of a modified session, for instance when people collaborate on a project by returning updated copies of an original session file.

[2]We take the opportunity to suggest a tip to import the automation in *overlay*: the session we are importing from must have a start ("Session Start") that is subsequent to that of the automation we want to keep.

consolidating, obtain just one new clip that is the daughter of the new and consolidated file conveniently created by Pro Tools.

"Consolidate" is a fairly inelegant command that can almost always be avoided by using the *clip group* mechanism (which we will see on 5.1, page 58) and/or the automation, which can both be edited non-destructively. If you really want to use this command you should at least copy the material to be consolidated onto another empty track and set it on *mute*, so you can step back to it if necessary.

"Mute" silences the clips contained in the current selection. Repeating the command will cause these clips to toggle back to the normal state, and in fact in that case the command name changes to "Unmute".

"Strip Silence" is a command that in some cases turns out to be very valuable, significantly speeding up otherwise repetitive operations. It lets you remove silences inside a clip and then break it into smaller clips that can be individually edited.

We have to specify the *threshold* level below which Pro Tools considers the signal to be silence, as well as minimum durations for the operation to take place and *handles* to be taken into account to prevent cutting too near the edge of the used sound material and so risking, for example, snipping off the reverb tails. The effect of the modifications on the parameters is shown live.

Though created to remove silences, hence the name, it can also perform the inverse operation[3] ("Extract" button) or simply perform cuts without removing anything ("Separate" button).

Automation commands The *automation*, which we have seen in 2.3, page 22, has come to be considered as essential

---

[3]The "Strip Silence" command can be useful, for example, in the research of *room tone*, or conversely to identify the highest peaks.

in mixing because it is non-destructive and avoids the necessity of physically recording partial mixes.

We have to bring your attention here to some limitations imposed by *Avid*'s commercial choices, limitations that are present in the non-HD versions with no *Complete Production Toolkit*. Specifically, the command "Write to All Enabled" will not be present, which would in one stroke write the present state of all automated parameters contained in the selection.

Tip on how
to write the
automation
In fact, with a trick it is possible to achieve something equivalent: put the relevant tracks in automation write mode then play for a few seconds at the head of the chosen selection and again at the tail, then remove all intermediate automation breakpoints of all automated parameters with the command "Clear Special"->"All Automation". It is not very handy but it turns out to be extremely useful when you have to work on a long selection and don't want to wait for it to play through.

"Fades" is a submenu that contains the commands related to the creation and editing of *fade-ins*, *fade-outs*, and *crossfades*. We will not linger long here, leaving the reader with the pleasure of exploration. We certainly advise committing to memory the [COMMAND] + [CTRL] +F shortcut, which creates a fade using the "Default Fade Settings" set in the preferences.

Here too there are some details that are worthwhile mentioning. Note for example that it is possible to generate fades and crossfades simultaneously for all the clips included in the selection; that the point of intersection in the crossfade can be set at -3 dB (*equal power*), suitable to cross clips that are not *phase coherent*, or at -6 dB (*equal gain*) for clips that are *phase coherent* (this covers the case of fades between contiguous material jumping from one track to another); and that it can also be set to free (*none*), which allows the independent dragging of the fade-in and fade-out curves thanks to the [OPTION] key.

Finally, we add that the seemingly useless rectangular-shaped *crossfade* can be useful to merge two clips as if they were two independent tracks, without any attenuation at the intersection.

"View" **Menu** is obviously related to display options that are all intuitive, especially when you dedicate a few seconds to practise with them. Let's comment on three commands:

"Narrow Mix" Narrows the appearance of the mixer modules, allowing more of them to be displayed in the *mix window*.

"Clip" The "Original Time Stamp" command contained in this submenu shows the original timecode location (known as *original time stamp*) for the first sample of each of the session's clips. In fact each time a file is created by consolidating, by using "AudioSuite" commands, or by recording, the file keeps track of the position in time of its first sample, which is enough for the system to know the subsequent position in time of any other audio sample.

"Sends A-E, Sends F-J" This allows the choice of whether to show all the sends or just one for each group of five, with the advantage to this last case being that there is enough space for a small *fader* to be shown, along with a small knob for the *panpot*, the small *mute* and *pre-fader* buttons, and a *level indicator* (if the related preference is switched on).

"Track" **Menu** Many of the its commands act instantaneously on the selected tracks. Some of them are very intuitive, others too advanced for our present purposes. Let's comment on the following two:

"Make Inactive" Allows the complete and reversible disabling of the selected tracks, which frees the processors from the related workload, especially as far as the plug-ins are concerned, and releases the drives from the burden of reading the files. It is clearly possible to re-enable such tracks by repeating the command, which in the meantime will have changed to "Make Active".

"Auto Input Monitoring" This command puts Pro Tools in this monitoring mode, and causes the opposite command of "Input Only Monitoring" to become instantly available in its place. We mentioned this on 2.2, page 17.

"Clip" **Menu** This is related to the clips selected in the tracks. Let's see three special commands:

Clip Group

"Group", "Ungroup", "Regroup" It is possible to create groups made of clips, fades, and gaps, even when they belong to different tracks and whether they are contiguous or not. This *clip group* is in fact a virtual box that appears to be a unique element but that can be made up of a complex combination of edits, even including other *clip groups*.

It will be possible to edit them as though dealing with normal clips, to apply cuts and fades and export the definition of these groups for later use in other sessions. Let's consider the clip grouping as a sort of virtual and reversible consolidation.

"Identify Sync Point" As already explained (3.1, page 26), this command allows an internal point in a clip to be defined that will be useful for synchronisation later on. The *sync point* so defined is shown as a small green triangle whose point is resting on the base of the rectangle surrounding the clip (item 11 in figure 3.1, page 30).

"Elastic Properties" This falls under the management of a relatively recent and not fully ripe function that allows sound to be treated as though it were elastic, permitting a surgical *stretching* (the sound quality so obtained must be carefully checked). They are anyway advanced and complex functions that lie outside our purposes and into which we leave the interested reader to delve.

"Event" **Menu** This relates to *MIDI*, a side to Pro Tools that we have chosen mostly to omit in this general understanding of the system.

There are two ways to manipulate musical timing, both modifying the bars/beats timeline and acting on the length of *MIDI*

Figure 5.1: The EQ III equaliser provided with Pro Tools is available in 1, 4 and 7-band, mono and stereo configurations.

events. The last command of this menu is the unavoidable "All MIDI Notes Off".

"AudioSuite" **Menu** Gathers the plug-ins in their file-based version and normally shows them divided into categories (*EQ, dynamics, pitch shift, reverbs,* and so on) but it's possible to sort by manufacturer or with a flat list, accessing a specific option in the Display Preferences.

We will take a close look at some of the standard ones:

"EQ III 7-band" This is one of the most used multiband equalisers[4]. Let's go deep into some of its features, most of which will prove to be instructional in the use of other *AudioSuite* effects.

---

[4]With version 10, Avid complemented the *EQ III* with a four-band, two-filter equaliser and dynamic processor that takes advantage of the new *AAX* plug-in format. See figure 2.3, page 12.

In passing, we have already mentioned the upper grey area in the window that controls *AudioSuite*, when we spoke about the Signal Generator (see 4, page 38). We will add that it is possible to store the settings by creating what is called a *preset*; these presets can be kept in folders and recalled in sequence, to audition them quickly, with the "+" and "-" onscreen buttons or by calling up a window that contains an inventory of all the presets and choosing them individually. By using the "COMPARE" button it is easy to compare the initial settings of the parameters with those that have been modified.

We note other details: close to the input gain control (pay attention to the risk of clipping; see 9.2, page 112) there is a button for inverting the signal *polarity*, and you can numerically insert some values with the keyboard as well as specify the unit of measure to distinguish between *hertz* (type "h" after the number) and *kilohertz* (type "k"). Pressing the [COMMAND] key allows a more accurate movement of the continuous controls when you drag them (this is true also for any other slider or rotating knob, including mixer faders and panpots). A click while holding the [OPTION] key will return a control to its default value.

Automating
a plug-in

Other interesting features are available only when the effects are used in real time as mixer plug-ins. The controls have an *LED* that indicates their automation status. You can enable the automation of each parameter by clicking on it while holding the three modifier keys [CTRL], [OPTION], and [COMMAND]. There is a small button at the top right that allows the window to be made sticky (you have to click it and make it grey instead of red), so that it does not disappear when you open the window of another plug-in.

The real-time processing type can be *RTAS* and *AAX*, i.e. *native*, where the sound is processed by the computer's processor, or *TDM* and *AAX dsp*, where the sound is processed by the dedicated processors called *DSP* that are contained in one or more additional cards.

"Pitch Shift"->"Time Shift" It is important that you are clear
about the difference between *varispeed, time stretch,* and
pitch shift:

Varispeed slows down or speeds up sonic material and
so produces the same effect to decreasing or increasing tape speed in an analogue playback device, with
the consequent lowering or raising of the frequencies. For example, by slowing to half the playback
speed the length doubles and the frequencies lower
by an octave.

Time stretch instead magically allows the duration of a
sound to be changed while keeping the pitch unaltered.

Pitch shift does the opposite of the *time stretch,* i.e. it
keeps the duration unaltered while it modifies the
pitch.

These last two operations are algorithmically very complex and, depending on the amount of variation and the
quality of the plug-in, they tend to be detrimental as far
as the audio quality is concerned.

Avid's "Time Shift" plug-in, heir of the old Digidesign's
"Pitch Shift" and "Time Compression Expansion", allows
all three operations and produces a good result with
varispeed.

"Other"->"Gain" This command will often be most useful for
one of its secondary functions: the rapid scan of the
selected material in search of the maximum peak or the
RMS value[5]. The measure does not take into account
the automation of the track volume but does take into
account the *clip gain* introduced with Pro Tools 10.

"Options" **Menu** This is rich in many very critical and useful items.

"Destructive Record" Normally when Pro Tools is recording,
if what is being recorded affects clips that are already

---

[5]The *RMS* value in dB FS is not measured by Pro Tools according to the *AES* and
IEC recommendations, so for a sine wave with peak 0 dB we will obtain an *RMS*
value equal to approx -3 dB FS.

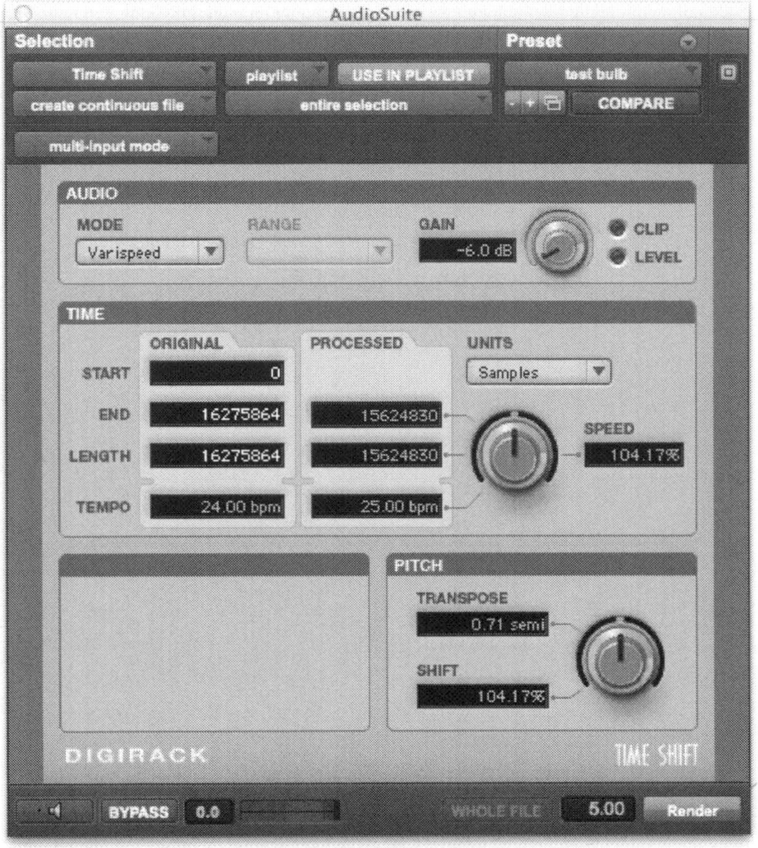

Figure 5.2: The "Time Shift" provided with Pro Tools.
To have a precision higher than three decimal points it is good to use the *sample* unit of measure and explicitly indicate the consequent length.
The gain has to be kept low as a precaution, to be raised subsequently with a compressor/limiter.
Note the multi-input mode, necessary to treat the various selected tracks as a single multichannel signal.

on the track it removes them from the track at that point, but the parent file is not touched. However, the dangerous option we are commenting on here enables irreversible *overwriting*.

The *destructive record* mode is useful when you want to restart after a break, without having to start over: you position the cursor a little before the spot where you stopped or the point to be modified and continue recording[6]. Pro Tools will resume writing the file from the point where it was stopped for your break.

This mode is highlighted by a "D" on the recording button of the transport commands.

"Transport Online" can be activated by a clock icon in the transport's panel. This ensures a synchronous link with the outside world by generating or receiving *timecode*, depending on whether Pro Tools is configured as *master* (*GEN LTC, GEN MTC, . . .*) or as *slave*.

Timecode

Managing the *timecode* in connection with external devices—through *MTC* (*Midi Time Code*) or other systems such as the *LTC* (*Longitudinal Time Code*) and the *biphase* if you own the *Sync I/O* interface—is an advanced operation that lies outside the purposes of this booklet.

"Video out Firewire" The video can be shown on a generic floating window on one of the computer screens (you show or hide it by entering [COMMAND]+9 on the numeric keypad; furthermore, you can manage the size by clicking on it with the right button of the mouse or while holding [CTRL] and clicking the left button, or even by dragging the edge) or sent to external video converters through the *firewire* port, when enabling this function. In any case, it will be important to line up audio and video with test signals and apply the proper time correction through the "Video Sync Offset. . ." from the "Setup" menu.

"Loop Playback" If the selection is not too short (longer than half a second, to be precise), when you enable this func-

---

[6]Note that you must enable a sufficient amount of *preroll* to catch the reverberation tail of sounds preceding the *punch-in* point.

tion and put the system in playback you will listen to the selection repetitively, as a *loop*. It is a useful mode when you want to find the right parameters for an effect (if they are automated, it is helpful to suspend automation).

"Edit Window Scrolling" Here you can choose how Pro Tools will behave when the cursor reaches the end of the editing window during playback or recording. There are four options: no reaction, the visible section shifting only once playback is stopped, a page change to display the following part of the edited tracks, and the far more handy and natural continuous scroll.

"Link Timeline and Edit Selection" I advise you to keep this option switched on. When disabled, the *start* and *end* cursors are doubled: one pair of cursors to indicate the playback time and one pair to select material for editing purposes.

"Automation Follows Edit" If this option is switched on, the *cut*, *copy* and *paste* commands, even if performed with the visualisation called *waveform*, act on the automation as well. It is an essential function when you modify material that has already been mixed.

"Pre Fader Metering" As we have already explained, the standard level-meters of each mixer module can be set to display what happens before or after the main fader and the main mute button action.

"Solo Mode" When you press the "Solo" key on a mixer module you automatically silence all the other modules except for those set on *solo safe*. Should you later press the "Solo" key of another module you will disengage the previous "Solo" if this option is set on "X-OR", or if this is set to "Latch" the previous *solo* will remain. The high-end Pro Tools systems allow other possibilities as well.

"Delay Compensation" This mode activates the automatic compensation of the delay (*latency*) that is created in the signal flow while it passes through the various stages of any digital audio workstation (*DAW*).

However, Pro Tools is not able to know at which points it is essential to line-up some tracks, nor can it automatically reconfigure the mixer when it proves mathematically impossible to line up two signals because one derives from the other. In other words, it is better for you to set the appropriate delays (using some "timeadjuster") manually and to configure the mixer so that the signals are lined up at the necessary points.

"Setup" **Menu** Allows the system to be configured and set for the optimal operation for typical use.

"Hardware..." From here you set all the characteristics of the physical input and output devices. What appears depends on the model of the chosen audio interface. For example, typically we will be able to choose if the optical interface has to behave according to the *S/PDIF* or *ADAT* specifications, and from where to take the *clock* (typically you choose among the port dedicated to the *word clock*, the internal quartz clock, or a clock that is rebuilt based on the flow of data received on a particular digital audio channel).

"Playback Engine..." With this we specify which audio interface (or, if using the "Pro Tools aggregate I/O", a combination of audio interfaces[7]) Pro Tools can access. It is also possible to set the size of the various buffers with which Pro Tools avoids being overwhelmed by audio data before it has finished with the previous lot, choose what percentage of the processing power of the computer's *CPU* to allocate, and decide whether to ignore system difficulties and let recording or playback proceed—but with the risk of suffering the effect of those errors (typically *digital clicks*) without being warned.

We are in truth entering the domain of the internal functionality of the system, in which the user ideally (!) should not be required to become involved. The general practical advice is to set medium or medium-high values and verify that the system proves to be suitable and stable for our typical needs, balancing through the

---

[7]Excluding in that case just the Avid-Digidesign ones, at least for now.

buffers for reliability on one side and responsiveness on the other.

Talking about *latency*, some hardware configurations allow a mode called "Low Latency Monitoring", which is useful to provide the performer, singer, or actor with a headphone cue (without a perceptible delay) of what they are doing.

✧

With Pro Tools it is advisable to set the system so that it does not put the computer or the drive to sleep or in other energy-saving modes.

✧

"Disk Allocation..." This is used to manage the assigning of the drives to the different tracks, so sharing the work-load on different devices to ensure performances that would be adequate for the parallel recording of a con-siderable number of tracks. This assigning is valid also for the creation of fades (in versions previous to 10, in fact, they are pre-calculated audio files and placed in the specific folder(s) linked to the tracks) and new files generated by commands in the "AudioSuite" menu or through consolidating.

"Peripherals..." This command makes a window pop up that contains several options. These options relate to synchro-nising (*timecode* managing) with external devices and their transports (*machine control*); configuring *control surfaces* (the part of the mixer that represents the inter-face with the operator) linked via *ethernet, USB, firewire, MIDI,* etc.; configuring other Pro Tools systems that man-age high-resolution video (*video satellite*); configuring the connection with *Avid Venue* mixing systems.

"I/O..." The configuration of *inputs, outputs,* and *buses* is accessible through a two-dimensional matrix that assigns them, placed on the horizontal axis, while the *paths* created by the user are placed on the vertical axis instead. Through the subpage related to the *inserts* it is possible to create the related *paths* that define them as pairs of *outputs* and *inputs* (it is mandatory to use the same numeration, so if we decide to exit on channels 3 and 4, Pro Tools will expect to receive the signal treated by the stereo device through inputs 3 and 4).

Subpaths (see the figure 2.1, page 9) can be defined by selecting a path and pressing the "New Subpath" button. A small triangle on the left of the *path* will allow the related *subpaths* to be seen or not. We remind you that they can be useful, for example, to access directly only the left and right outputs or only the channel dedicated to the subwoofer in a 5.1 path (more than 2-track configurations are available on Pro Tools HD systems or adding the *Complete Production Toolkit*).

In the output subpage we find two important options: "Audition Paths", which allows you to define the channels that Pro Tools will be using for the preview on different occasions, and "Session overwrite current I/O Setup when opened", which it is advisable to leave switched on, otherwise the I/O configuration will remain at the previous session's settings even if you open a new session that expects a totally different configuration, with consequences that would be difficult to manage.

"Video Sync Offset..." This allows the insertion of a delay on the audio related to the *video track*, with quarter-frame steps, i.e. ten milliseconds in the case of a *PAL* format video. Positive values that delay the audio to the video or negative values that advance the audio to the video are possible.

Audiovisual system line up

To calibrate your system you can use a change of frame that is particularly evident (from a dark scene to a light scene, for example) and from that same spot put a three- or four-second tone that you can use to verify by sight, over and over, the simultaneity of the change of frame and the beginning of the tone. A better result is guaranteed by looking at the video with the corner of your eye. Obviously the test must be done from the spot where the subject normally watches and listens, bearing in mind that three and a half meters of distance already implies a ten-millisecond delay in the sound.

It is not claimed that the system remains stable at each playback and so the calibration must be verified frequently, for example at the beginning of each work day.

"Session" Since version 10 it has become possible to use audio files with different formats, sample frequencies, and bit depths in the same session. With this command you can set the characteristics that Pro Tools will use when recording and generating audio files.

The "Session Start" value determines through an offset the relation between time positions expressed in *samples* or *minutes and seconds* (and milliseconds), which always start at nought on the far left of the timeline, and the values expressed as *timecode*. When modifying its value we will be asked whether to keep the audio clips, fades, *MIDI* clips, and automation at the previous *timecode* or instead to maintain the position relative to the beginning of the session. Sometimes this last option is the only one possible due to the presence of *markers*, changes in *tempo*, clips, or automation points in an area that would end up being deleted.

The "Timecode Rate" defines the number of parts into which a second is divided when you use the *timecode* to express time positions. In Europe, for example, it is typical to divide the second in 25 parts as a technical consequence of the choice of 50 Hz for the frequency of the electricity supply. In USA and Japan the NTSC system uses 29.97 frames per second.

The *timecode rate* must not be confused with the concept of *film speed* that involves a changes of durations.

"Current Time Code Position..." We have just seen that the *time ruler* starts with a *timecode* that can be defined by the user. With this command it is possible to easily move the ruler so that the spot where the cursor is ends up to be at the required *timecode* value, and obviously Pro

Tools will shift the position of the whole edited session accordingly.

"MIDI"->"MIDI Studio..." This calls up the operating-system application that manages the general audio and *MIDI* configuration.

"Preferences..." To these, which are plenty, we have dedicated chapter 6, page 75.

"Window" **Menu** This concerns the displaying of the various windows. First of all we remind you of the very important and very often used keyboard shortcut that lets you toggle from the *edit window* to the *mix window* and vice versa: [COMMAND]+=.

Let's now comment on some commands:

"Configurations" Allows the layout of the Pro Tools windows to be saved, including the floating ones, and their particular configurations to be quickly recalled.

"Task Manager" This reveals a window showing all the background operations, such as

- the *fade rendering* when, on opening session, Pro Tools (previous to 10) could not find the fades so you decided to let it render them again,
- a search for audio files it did not find in the folder where it expected to find them,
- the calculation of the graphics related to the *waveforms*.

It is possible to pause these tasks to avoid overloading the system, particularly during playback or recording.

Explore, related to this, the pop up menu that can be called up with a click on the round button with a triangle, at the top right.

"Workspace" This reveals a browser for the audio that uses a dedicated database called *DigiBase*.

From the main workspace window you can set the drives, enabling them for playback, record (and playback), or defining them as transit drives, respectively selecting "P",

"R", or "T". Searches can then be performed using the internal metadata of the files, such as the recording's start *timecode* (*original time stamp*) and the creation date. A right-click on the title of one of the columns will display a list of the countless others that can be activated and used for searching as well. You can also move the columns between the left and right halves of the window.

"Project" This is very similar to "Workspace" but is restricted to the files involved in the current session, showing them all in one folder even if they are scattered in different locations, or even on different drives.

"Automation" This causes a small window to appear that allows the reading/writing of the automation to be enabled or suspended, which can be global or limited to only the writing of the movements of the *faders*, of the *panpots*, of the main or send *mutes*, or any other automated parameters of any of the *plug-ins*[8].

"Memory Locations" This shows the list of all the memory locations generated with the [RETURN] key on the numeric keypad, as explained on 4.1, page 45.

It is possible to access a specific pop-up menu, as well as sift the view according to the memory types, for example showing only the ones with a time position (*Markers*) or only the ones that recall the display (*show/hide*) of some tracks (you have to click on the eye-shaped icon). Clicking on a *memory location* in this window while holding [OPTION] will delete it, while with [CTRL] it can be redefined.

"Color Palette" You can colour the tracks and individual clips. See the related preferences explained in 6.1, page 76.

"Marketplace" **Menu** Introduced with Pro Tools 10 this allows pages on the Web to be accessed, such as those for the plug-ins, virtual instruments, and other *Avid* or third party add-ons.

---

[8]On bigger systems when you click on "SUSPEND" while holding the modifier [COMMAND] only the automation of the *trim* values is suspended.

"Help" **menu** This is useful, for example, to view the reference manual, or the document that summarises the keyboard shortcuts. There is also a command to check for software updates.

5.2 Clip list menu

By clicking on the small button on the right of the word *CLIPS*, in the area immediately above the list of clips in the right column of the *edit window*, you can access an essential pop up menu for which we describe, as usual, only the most important items:

"Find. . . " This performs a selective sifting of the clips, showing only the ones that contain the text we type. The sifted visualisation is highlighted by the fact that the word *CLIPS* is followed by the search text, in square brackets. It is clearly possible to return the list to its normal state with the "Clear Find" command.

We point out that the *auto-created clips* are shown or hidden according to a preference that we will see in the next command, and it is good to take this into account when we want to remove the unused clips from the session.

"Show. . . " Among other things this allows the name of the parent file, disk name, or even the whole pathname[9] (by activating "Full Path") to be seen in front of each clip. This last option turns out to be useful when sorting by disk name: a quick glance at the *clip list* will be reassuring should you have to move your work and be certain that the chosen device contains all the necessary files, without having to bother the slow "Save Copy In. . . " command.

To understand the "Auto Created" option we have to take a step back: when you define a new clip inside a larger clip Pro Tools could ask what name to give it or automatically assign one, according to a preference, while the two clips that are necessarily created on the left and right always receive an

---

[9]The *pathname* is nothing but the path through directories and subdirectories to reach the file starting from the root of the drive structure.

automatic name. These two clips are *auto(matically) created* and it is possible to show or hide them in the *clip list*.

"Select"->"Unused" This selects the clips that have not been used in the editing. This is normally the waiting room of their deletion by giving a command that we are about to see. As said, we have to mind the fact that the auto-created clips may not be visible and so not selected by this command.

"Sort by..." This sets the sorting criterion for the display of the *clip list*. Sorting the clips by *original time stamp* can be useful when looking for material that has been recorded approximately around the same *timecode* of a clip; while sorting by creation date of the parent file can prove handy to highlight clips pertaining to recently created files.

"Clear..." This removes the selected clips from the list. If a clip entirely coincides with the whole of its parent file (in which case it will be written in bold) we can choose whether to remove just the clip or to delete its parent file from the drive as well; it is obviously a dangerous operation and one to be evaluated properly because the same parent file could have other daughter clips, which are used in other sessions that would not be able to find the deleted file.

"Compact..." This is used to reduce the size of the parent files by analysing which clips are their daughters and cutting the parents accordingly (at the heads and tails only!). Rarely used and potentially dangerous.

"Export Clip Definitions..." The definition of the clip is contained in the session, not in the parent file. This command causes those definitions to be incorporated within the parent file, so that when importing the file in another session it is possible to see its partitioning into various clips that can be individually imported.

"Export Clips as Files..." This allows the creation in different formats of various parallel mono files or an interleaved file for each of the clips selected in the *clip list*. Before version 10, Pro Tools used to worked only with mono files, one for each channel, while almost all audio playback devices expect an interleaved[10] file (all the channels are inside a single file).

It is possible to perform re-sampling at different frequencies, re-quantisation with different bit-depth, and also *MP3* encoding. Pro Tools asks the user what quality to use to perform the conversions, obviously at the expense of the time needed to perform the operation: we strongly suggest that you perform some trials and judge the effect by ear with a good set of headphones, particularly for the *MP3* conversion with respect to the algorithms adopted by other programs.

"Export Clip Groups" Once one *clip group* has been defined (see 5.1, page 58) it could be useful to make it available to other sessions. This command simply allows that.

"Timeline Drop Order" This allows the choice, when dragging multiple material from other programs or from the *clip list* on the *timeline*, of whether such material is to be distributed by Pro Tools on different tracks, so from top to bottom, or in sequence on the time axis on one track only, from left to right.

5.3 Contextual menus

These are special menus generally accessible through the right button of the mouse or with the usual click together with a modifying key (on Mac OS X it is [CTRL]). They appear relative to the clicked point and, as the name suggests, present commands that pertain to the object to be found there. We name only a few among the most useful:

1. On the track or related mixer module name: allows commands such as "Hide", "Make Inactive", "Duplicate...", "Split into Mono", and "Delete...".

2. On the recording button of the transport window: a menu appears that lets you select, for example, the *destructive record* mode that is highlighted with the letter "D" superimposed on the button.

---

[10]Obviously when playing back an *interleaved*—also called *interlaced*—file the audio samples are first lined up and then sent out simultaneously.

3. On the empty space at the top right of the edit window or on the small button shown as item 16 in figure 3.1, page 30: it makes some elements in that area appear or disappear, for example the transport commands and the buttons that generate *timecode* signals of various kinds.

4. On a clip: this allows the "Snap to Next" or "Snap to Previous" commands to be given.

5. On the video window: this is where to decide the size of the frame.

CHAPTER 6

Exploring the Preferences

Pro Tools preferences are recalled with the command found in the "Setup" menu that makes a window appear where, based on their function, the preferences are gathered into seven subpages: "Display", "Operation", "Editing", "Mixing", "Processing", "MIDI", and "Synchronization".

As we did for the commands, we will focus only on those items that we consider to be the more important, the most dangerous, and/or the least intuitive.

6.1 Display

This page's preferences concern some aspects of the display. Let's see the two most useful ones:

Meters Pro Tools meters[1] can memorise the maximum peak reached and highlight it with a permanently lit dash.

It is also possible to see a numeric measure: while holding the [COMMAND] key just click on the decibel indication of the main fader's position on the mixer module in which we

---

[1]There are many plug-ins that can be used as alternatives, which are able to measure the signal by analysing the *intrasample peak*, also called *true peak*, the *RMS* value using a choice of weighting curves, and the *loudness* measured with different algorithms. Unfortunately they do not replace the basic Pro Tools meters on the screen or on the consoles, and so require space on the monitor screen.

are interested. Having done so, you can cycle through three indications: the fader position that controls the gain, the maximum peak reached, and the undesired delay between input signal and output signal, known as *latency*, which is due to the signal processing time needed for plug-ins and the general functioning of the system.

These three layers of the numeric display are indicated respectively by the abbreviations *vol*, *pk*, and *dly*, which are visible if "Narrow Mix" in the "View" menu is disabled.

With the preferences for the meters we can set how often the memory of maximum peak ("Peak Hold") is reset to $-\infty$ dB, if at all. The choice is between "None" (the function is completely disabled), "3 Seconds", and "Infinite"—in which case the meters are reset manually by clicking on them.

With "Clip Indication" we can ask Pro Tools to use a red indicator to highlight when we have reached 0 dB FS (Full Scale), as exceeding this level is a dangerous situation for fixed-point audio files, physical input- and output-ports, and non-AAX plug-ins (see 9.2, page 108).

The settings we suggest are "3 Seconds" for the "Peak Hold" function, because this value helps to identify the channels that were modulating when playback stopped, and "Infinite" for clipping, given the severity of this condition.

Color Coding The preferences concerning the colouring of *markers*, *tracks*, and *clips* are found in this area. By setting "Default Track Color Coding" on "None" and "Default Clip Color Coding" on "Track Color" we will prevent Pro Tools from automatically colouring tracks and clips according to its own criteria, and instead leave that up to us.

For example we can colour the tracks (and related clips) red that are dedicated to recording a mix, dialogues in blue, music tracks in magenta, and the effects in yellow. We can even choose a sequence of eight repeated colours to be associated with the faders of a control surface, to quickly identify the track and the related mixer module; a "magic" sequence is: 1) blue, 2) red, 3) green, 4) orange, 5) purple, 6) dark yellow, 7) light blue, and finally 8) magenta.

Eight
colours

6.2 Operation

This page describes some special preferences that affect how Pro Tools responds to our actions.

Transport We advise you to keep the "Timeline Insertion/Play Start Marker Follows Playback" option switched on, so that when the playback is stopped the cursor is moved to the last point to have been played and does not return to the point where the playback started. It is probably the most logical and useful setting, although special needs might cause you to decide otherwise.

Numeric Keypad The numeric keypad that is present on the majority of the computer keyboards in Pro Tools can be used in different ways. By setting the behaviour to "Classic" it will be possible to recall a *memory location* by simply typing its identifying number on the numeric keypad, followed by a decimal point. This proves to be very useful to recall the display of a certain group of tracks on which we want to focus, often when the session is particularly rich and complex.

Another feature of the "Classic" mode is that by pressing the numeric keypad figures together with the modifying key [CTRL] you can play a track at different speeds. Try for example with [CTRL]+3, then 4, 5 for normal speed, and so on speeding up, with "+" and "-" affecting the direction of the playback.

Enable Session File Auto Backup The automatic save-to-disk mechanism is not sufficiently sophisticated to allow complete peace Backup of mind. We suggest you integrate it by duplicating a session before opening it, so having a snapshot of the situation at the beginning of the day, for example, and for each day of work. For greater security we advise that you backup to another drive or to the cloud[2].

---

[2]The Mac OS X operating system currently presents some useful functions that can memorise previous versions of a document (called *Versions*, and which we hope will soon be implemented by Pro Tools), as well as recover mistakenly deleted material (*Time Machine*).

Record In this section of the preferences we find first the option "Latch Record Enable Buttons", which allows the buttons that arm the tracks not to be disabled as we press another button of the same kind on another module.

With "Link Record and Play Faders" we can make Pro Tools remember different positions for the fader depending on whether a track is armed or not[3].

Using the "Online" options we can define whether the recording must start as soon as the external *timecode* is locked or wait until it reaches the position of the Pro Tools start cursor.

Recording
space
allocation

Talking about "Open-Ended Record Allocation", if the option "Use All Available Space" is selected, when Pro Tools begins recording it asks the operating system to allocate the entire free space of the drive/s involved. Once the recording process is concluded, any unused parts of the drive become available again. This operation generally leads to a waiting time that can be sensibly reduced by declaring that we do not want to record for more than a certain amount of minutes, which can be set with the other option, aptly called "Limit to ... minutes". However, the risk is that the recording could be stopped too soon or in an unsuitable place, for example during the unforeseen encore of an internationally famous artist during their farewell concert. It is a good habit to check this preference before you record an important event.

6.3 Editing

That is, preferences related to editing.

Clips When the preference "Clip List Selection Follows Edit Selection" is enabled, selecting a clip on a track will automatically select it on the *clip list*. Another preference, found directly below, will enable the opposite: selecting a clip from the clip list will automatically cause the first occurrence of that clip to become selected on the track. Generally, leave both switched on.

---

[3] An advanced trick is to use this option to create an *intercom* inside Pro Tools, so avoiding an interruption in playback when in STOP or a double playback occurring while recording. We will talk about this in a future book.

Memory Locations The preference "Auto/Name Memory Locations when Playing" allows markers to be created on the timeline without being interrupted by the window that asks for a name and other characteristics. It turns out to be essential, for example, when you mark the *beat* by ear using the [RETURN] key on the numeric keypad, to be able to perform rhythmically correct cuts later on.

Fades In this section we can set the *fades default type* Pro Tools will apply when you use the shortcut [COMMAND]+[CTRL]+F or the *smart tool*.

6.4 Mixing

That is, preferences related to mixing.

Setup The "Link Mix/Edit Groups Enables" is a noteworthy item: it automatically links the enabling and disabling of corresponding mixing and editing groups in the mix and edit windows.

Automation It is time to delve into some general issues related to automation, which we introduced in 2.3.

To begin, let's note that in *touch* and *latch* mode the system must be aware that we are touching a control before it will begin to start recording our operations on that control. This is easy for the system when physical controllers are moved, but when they are touched and held stationary it becomes necessary to have controls (faders and rotating knobs) that are able to sense contact with the user's body. These controls are obviously more expensive than the regular ones, so much so that the budget control surfaces usually have this function on faders only.

Touch-Sensitive Controls

While in *touch* mode the absence of touch sensitivity can be compensated for by acquiring the habit of very slightly but continually adjusting the control whose movement you are recording: this prevents Pro Tools from believing that we have released the control and so it contues to write instead of returning to reading previously written automation.

The *switch* controls too have their own specific issues that justify special solutions, which accounts for the presence of preferences such as "Latching Behavior for Switch Controls in Touch".

When a control is not touched anymore, if we are in *touch* mode, the system will revert to read the previous automation; you usually do not want this to happen immediately, as it would create a disagreeable and often audible step, but rather over a period of time that can be set by the user by the "AutoMatch Time" option. A 1,500 millisecond value will turn out to be appropriate in most cases. The risk of setting higher values is that you can forget that the released control is "gliding" towards the previous automation point and you press *stop* without waiting for its conclusion, thereby unwillingly creating that same automation step that you wanted to avoid.

To close, let's comment on the "After Write Pass, Switch to:". This protects us from the damages of forgetting that a module is in automation *write* mode: you can set an automatic switch from *write* mode to something less dangerous, such as *touch* or *latch*, that will happen upon the command to stop.

Controllers Aside from the "Touch Timeout" controls that we just mentioned, to understand this group of preferences we need to highlight the fact that usually the control surfaces have a lesser number of physical modules (*channel strips*) than Pro Tools could potentially manage, and so Pro Tools allows the rapid reassignment of the physical mixer modules to pages (*banks*) of virtual mixer modules. The most advanced control surfaces also allow such pages to be freely specified by rearranging the sequence of the desired modules independently from their arrangement on the *mix window* and on the *edit window* (*custom faders* on *D-Control*).

Some of the preferences in this section link the vertical scroll of the edit window and the horizontal scroll of the mix window to the selection of the control surface banks made by the sound engineer.

6.5 Processing

That is, preferences related to actions on the files. In regard to some of these related to *dither*[4], we suggest you delve into them at another time because they are of considerable technical complexity.

Import The preference "Automatically Copy Files on Import" prevents, when set, the existence of files used by our session that reside outside the related *Audio Files* folder associated with the track involved (through the command "Disk Allocation..."). This way Pro Tools creates and uses a copy of the imported files. In the case of large files, however, this could lead to an inefficient use of disk space[5].

We already mentioned the choices relating to audio quality that can be set while performing some operations. In the specific case that pertains to the "Sample Rate Conversion Quality" we advise against any saving (in the end the computer does not sweat) and instead to select the maximum value, which is "TweakHead (Slowest)".

TC/E Plug-in With the *trim tool* in its alternative version (to select it, you have to click and hold on this tool's icon: a watch with the word *TCE*) that allows *time stretching*, you can modify the length of a clip without modifying its *pitch*.

We suggest you to review what was said in 5.1, page 61 in relation to the "Time Shift" *AudioSuite* command. Because it is so easy to ruin the quality of the sound with this kind of command, we recommend that you use them carefully.

You can choose here the algorithm and parameter presets that Pro Tools should use, which is useful if you have bought powerful *AudioSuite* plug-ins as alternatives to those included.

---

[4]Dither is a special decorrelating noise helping to hide the quantisation distortion. I suggest the very well written "Dither Explained" article by Nika Aldrich.

[5]Unfortunately there isn't a command that would gather all the files used by a session in only one folder without copying them but just by moving their locations (which is clearly possible only when the two locations are in the same *volume*).

CHAPTER 7

Using the Keyboard

We have already mentioned some keyboard commands and indicated how to deliver them by using the appropriate combination of keys.

Some operations are used so often that it is impractical not to know the equivalent shortcuts. Accordingly, below you will find those that we consider to be the most important ones and our advice is to memorise them. For specific cases it will be necessary to consult the "Pro Tools Shortcuts" document that can be called-up from the "Help" menu.

We recommend that you use an extended keyboard containing a numeric keypad.

7.1 Conventions

Though we have introduced them already, we want to remind you here about some particularly important conventions.

1. The "+" symbol indicates that a combination of keys should be pressed and held in sequence. Modifying keys must be pressed before the key they modify and released immediately afterwards.

2. As usual, the term *click* signifies the pressing and immediate release of the mouse's main button (usually the left one) or the equivalent action on the trackpad.

3. *Drag* means sliding with the pointing device (mouse or track-pad) while holding down the left button or equivalent, and *drag and drop* is used for when you move an object by grabbing it and releasing it at a precise point.

4. The symbol "/" is usually indicated with the name *slash* and its mirror image "\" is called a *backslash*.

5. What we indicate with [OPTION] on Mac is also sometimes called [ALT]. The icon on the key is a bit like a railway switch, just to indicate that it is usually associated with alternatives.

6. If the mouse or the trackpad doesn't have a right button, or the button is inactive, use the left button together with the modifier [CTRL] key.

7. Sometimes to indicate a comma, a full stop, an equals sign, or other signs, for greater clarity the name is written in full between the major and lesser symbols, so for example instead of "[COMMAND]+," we write "[COMMAND]+ <comma>".

8. The equivalent on a *Windows* keyboard is:

   • use [CTRL] where you read [COMMAND];

   • use [START], the key with the *Window*'s logo, where you read [CTRL].

7.2 Essential shortcuts

[OPTION]

Applies some of the operations to all the elements at once. For example it's useful to select the elements, to arm the tracks, mute them, insert *plug-ins*, assign *inputs* and *outputs*, create *sends*, change the height of the tracks, and choose the automation mode. However, when clicking on continuous controls such as *knobs*, *faders*, and *sliders* it will return them to the *default* value.

It is also useful for duplicating *clips* by dragging those already on the tracks, and to duplicate *sends* or *inserts* by dragging them from one *mixer module* to another.

In other cases it is used to generate an alternative operation, typically to achieve the opposite of that which is customarily associated with a particular action.

[OPTION]+[SHIFT]

Behaves in a similar way to the previous shortcut applying some operations to many elements, but only affects the selected ones.

[SHIFT]

Allows a selection to be extended, defining one end when the other end has already been defined. It is possible to select contiguous tracks by clicking on the name of the first track and then pressing [SHIFT] while clicking on the name of the last track, and for selections on the editing area when dragging proves to be cumbersome given the range of the desired selection: a click on one end is followed by a [SHIFT]+click on the other.

[COMMAND]

This allows a fine adjustment when dragging on continuous parameters such as *faders* and *panpots*, as well as the frequencies, gains, and slopes in the equalisers, and the ratio, threshold, and times in compressors, etc. The increased accuracy is also valid when moving automation points. Furthermore, it allows you to add and remove items from a multiple selection. For example should you want to select all the tracks up to 32, except 12 and further including 43, you would use the [SHIFT] as described above to select from one to 32 and then use [COMMAND]+click on track 12 to deselect it and again on 43 to include it with the others.

[CTRL]

Allows you to assign more than one output to a mixer module by selecting the additional outputs while holding [CTRL]. Pro Tools indicates the multiple-output status with a little "+" in the small rectangular area related to the chosen output.

It is also used when moving continuous controls or when clicking on buttons that affect a *mix group*, so that the link with the same control on the other mixer modules of the group is temporarily ignored.

[SPACEBAR]

Puts the system in playback or stops the system if it's already playing back or recording. Adding the modifying [COMMAND] key will cause Pro Tools to start recording (more precisely the armed tracks will record and the others will playback).

<Left arrow>

This moves the display of the *edit window* so that the selection's *start* cursor is in the centre of the window. Use the <right arrow> and Pro Tools will do the same for the selection's *end* cursor.

[COMMAND] + [OPTION] + <REWIND>	Valid only on high-specs systems, this rewinds the playback head by an amount (typically of about six seconds) set in the preferences, before resuming (or starting, if the system was in stop) playback. This function is called "Back and Play" and is very useful when we want to go back and correct a mistake. <REWIND> button can be found in the transport's floating window, the transport on the control surface, or the *edit window* (if hidden, we can make it appear by pressing the right button of the pointing device in the empty area to the right of the meters in the edit window).
[COMMAND] + click on the *solo* button	Enables or disables a track's *solo safe*, which is a function that prevents a mixer module from being muted when the *solo* button on another module is pressed.
[COMMAND] + click on the <REC enable button>	Enables or disables the *rec safe* of a track, which is a function that prevents the track from being accidentally armed.
[COMMAND] + <full stop>	Interrupts the recording and discards what has been recorded.
[COMMAND] + K	Enables/disables *pre-roll* and *post-roll*[1].

---

[1] Sometimes we accidentally enable a huge *pre-roll* and don't realise why the playback begins at a point that is a long way from the cursor.

Number followed by <period>, all on the numerical keypad	By typing a number on the numerical keypad, concluded with <period>, you can recall the *memory location* associated with that number (one or more digits are allowed). It proves to be very useful for recalling specific displays (see 4.1, page 45) such as all the dialogue, sound effects, or music tracks when mixing a film. The numeric keypad must be set to *classic mode* in the preferences.
[CTRL]+*drag and drop*	Temporarily transforms the *selector* tool into a *scrubber*.
[COMMAND]+1 or 2, 3, 4, 5, 6	Selects specific tools, respectively the *zoomer, trim, selector, grabber, scrubber,* or *pencil*. You could equally use the function keys from F5 onwards providing they are not assigned to other functions of the operating system, or you could repeatedly press the [ESC] key.

[TAB]

Moves the cursor to the next location, be that the next *sync point*
or the beginning or end of a *clip*
or a *fade*, or if the cursor is on the
marker ruler it will jump to the
next *marker*.

When used in conjunction with
the modifying [OPTION] key it
moves the cursor in the opposite
direction.

If the "Tab to Transients" option is
active it identifies the transients
and positions itself there, which is
a very handy function for editing
percussion instruments or more
generally on recordings that have
well-defined transients.

[CTRL] + [TAB]

Selects the next *clip* whereas combining it with the [OPTION] key
selects the previous *clip*.

[SHIFT] + [TAB]

Extends the selection moving the
end cursor to the next location, be
that a *sync point*, the end of the
current *clip* or *fade*, or the start of
the next *clip* or *fade*. Combined
with the [OPTION] key the selection extends in the opposite direction.

[RETURN]	Takes the (double) cursors back to the beginning of the session. Combined with the [OPTION] key the cursor moves to the end of the session instead. Finally, adding the modifying [SHIFT] key, as already explained, moves only one of the two cursors and so extends the selection to the beginning or the end of the session.
[RETURN] on the numeric keypad	Creates a new *memory location* whether the system is in stop, playback, or record mode, as described in 4.1, page 45. On compact keyboards you can often use a combination of keys such as [fn]+[RETURN].
Double click on a *clip* with the *selector*	Selects the whole *clip*.
Double click on the empty space between two *clips* with the *selector*	Selects the blank space.
Triple click with the *selector*, or [COMMAND]+A	Selects all the elements of a track, i.e. the beginning of the first *clip* to the end of the last. It is a very dangerous key combination because, if the *zoom* is such that it does not show the ends of a clip, you may not realise that you have made by mistake a *triple click* instead of a double click, and have consequently selected the whole track instead of a single *clip*.

[RETURN] followed by [COM-MAND]+A	Selects all the clips in all displayed tracks.
[SHIFT]+click on other tracks	Extends the selection to other tracks.
[COMMAND]+[OPTION]+ [CTRL]+ <up arrow> or <down arrow>	Resizes the tracks so that they are all contained in the vertical limits of the *edit window*.
[CTRL]+ <up arrow> or <down arrow>	Increases or decreases the vertical space dedicated to the tracks on which the cursor is placed.
[CTRL] while using the *trim tool*	Extends the *clip* to the following or previous *clip*'s edge.
[OPTION]+*drag and drop*	With the *grabber* tool this allows you to move what is selected by duplicating it, i.e. by leaving the original intact. Usefully, this applies to the *plug-ins, inserts* and *sends* too.
[DELETE]	Deletes that which is selected.
[CTRL]+click with the *grabber* on a *clip*	Moves the *clip* so that its head coincides with where the *start* cursor was positioned. Adding [COMMAND] instead moves the *clip* so that its tail coincides with the *end* cursor, or finally with [SHIFT] the *sync point* is aligned with the *start* cursor's position.

[CTRL]+drag and drop	As a side effect of the above and providing you have first selected the *clip* you want to move, or at least the *start* cursor is positioned exactly on the start of the *clip*, with this shortcut the clip's movement is restricted to the vertical, which is to say move it to another track while maintaining its position in time.
"+" and "-" keys on the numeric keypad (or [CTRL]+<full stop> and [CTRL]+<comma>)	Clips that are completely included in the selection are moved by the value set for the *nudge*, respectively delaying or advancing them in relation to the timeline. Providing there is sufficient material outside the *clip*'s start and end points, adding [CTRL] Pro Tools will slide the contents by the amount configured for the *nudge* value.
[CTRL]+P or <semicolon>	Moves the cursor to the track immediately above or below.
[OPTION]+A or double click on the *zoomer*	Causes the horizontal *zoom* to show the entire session and resets the vertical *zoom* to 100%, i.e. the vertical extremese of the audio waveform corresponding to 0 dB Full Scale Digital.
[COMMAND]+ <square brackets>	Performs a horizontal *zoom* in the *edit window*. By adding [OPTION] the *zoom* will be vertical instead, for all tracks.

[COMMAND]+click on a *zoom* preset button	Stores up to five *zoom* settings.
[CTRL]+1 ,2, 3, 4, 5	Recalls the stored *zoom* levels.
[COMMAND]+S	Saves, which is to say writes, the current state of the session onto the volume.
[COMMAND]+Z	The well-known "Undo", which, in case we reconsider an edit, allows us to go back one or more steps and remove the effect of the previous operations. See "Undo History" in the "Window" menu and the related preference that allows up to 32 steps back. By combining with the [SHIFT] modifier, you will obtain the undo of the undo, i.e. a "Redo".
[COMMAND]+X	Cuts the selected material by removing it and temporarily puts it in a parking spot (*clipboard*) from where we can subsequently paste it somewhere else with [COMMAND]+V.
[COMMAND]+C	Copies the selected material, as with the shortcut above, but leaves the original in place. As per the "Cut" command, the copied material is parked, waiting for an eventual command that would paste it somewhere.

[COMMAND]+V	Pastes the previously cut or copied material where the cursor is positioned. In cases where the material includes multiple tracks it will be necessary to span with the cursor a corresponding number of tracks into which an identical copy can be pasted.
[COMMAND]+A	Selects all the material on the track or tracks covered by where the cursor is positioned.
[COMMAND]+D	Duplicates the selected material and places it immediately after the selection. We once more remind you that all these operations act on *clips*, which are nothing but pointers to (portions of) *parent files*. Therefore duplicating a *clip* a thousand times means simply using a single portion of a single file a thousand times—no additional drive space is used.
[COMMAND]+E	Performs a *virtual cut* inside the *clip* where the cursor is located, cutting the *clip* in two (three if *start* and *end* cursors do not coincide). Such cuts can be healed with [COMMAND]+H, namely with the "Heal Separation" command.
[CTRL]+click on a *memory location* (on the *marker ruler* or on the dedicated window)	Allows you to change the *memory location*'s name, number, and other stored characteristics.

[OPTION]+click on a *memory location*	Deletes the *memory location*.
[COMMAND]+[OPTION]+/	Writes the current state of all automated parameters for the selection. It only works on HD or systems provided with *Complete Production Toolkit*. Because this command is so useful (and the toolkit so expensive) we remind you of the trick we mentioned on 5.1, page 56 to achieve the same on lower-grade systems.
[COMMAND]+[CTRL]+ click on a control	Visualises the control's automation lane. Try it on a *panpot* or a *fader*.
[COMMAND]+F	Creates a *fade* on the portion of the *clip* included in the selection (it doesn't matter whether the selection extends beyond the *clip* as this will not affect the duration of the *fade*). A window with the different types of curves and options will pop up.
[COMMAND]+[CTRL]+F	Creates a *fade* but instead of recalling the window with the different parameters it uses the settings we choose as *default* in the preferences (*Editing* subpage).
[COMMAND]+G	Creates a *mix group* and/or *edit group* that includes all the selected mixer modules.

[OPTION]+[SHIFT]+D	Duplicates the selected mixer modules.
[OPTION]+C	Resets all clipping indicators.
[COMMAND]+M	Mutes or unmutes all the clips that are entirely included in the selection.
[COMMAND]+[OPTION]+G	Creates an editing group, i.e. displays the selection as one "macro-clip" called a *clip group*. To ungroup it, use U ("Ungroup") instead of G ("Group").
[COMMAND]+<comma>	Defines a special point inside the *clip* that is called *sync point.*
[OPTION] clicking on a button of a dialog box	Extends the choice to all elements. For example, were you to decide to remove about a thousand clips from the *clip list*, many of which are used in the session, Pro Tools will ask if we are really sure we want to remove each one. Using the [OPTION] key removes the need to give the same answer over and over again.
[OPTION]+click on a *clip* in the *clip list*	Plays the *clip* through the *audition path* set in the *I/O Setup window*.
Double click on a *clip* with the *grabber*	Allows you to change the name of a *clip*. You can do this with any tool, not only the *grabber*, provided you click on the *clip list* instead of on the *clip* in the editing area.

[COMMAND]+[SHIFT]+G   Disables/enables all mix and edit groups.

[COMMAND]+<equal>   Toggles between the mix and edit windows.

[OPTION]+J   Brings all the different browser windows (for example, *workspace* and *project* windows) to the foreground.

<asterisk> on the numeric keypad   Activates the numeric input of the time position on the *main counter*, moving the (double) cursors accordingly. By pressing the <right arrow> or <left arrow> keys you move, for example, from minutes to seconds and so on. Once the value has been typed in just press [RETURN] to finish.

[CTRL]+D or G   Creates a *fade* in extending from the head of the *clip* to the cursor's position. Using G instead of D creates a *fade out* at its tail.

CHAPTER 8

Troubleshooting

The commercial choices of big companies are often more guided by the desire to increase functionality, which can be marketing oriented rather than strictly necessary, than by the will to invest in making their product more stable, getting rid of *bugs*, and improving the efficiency.

Pro Tools has grown year by year to incorporate ever more complex functions—such as *Elastic Audio* or the score notation inherited from the *Sibelius* software—than those for which it was initially made. Unfortunately you cannot expect complete reliability and therefore it is beneficial for critical and high-level work environments that a technical person is available who can quickly resolve technical difficulties and restore the smooth functioning of this complex system, or temporarily bypass problems while searching for a permanent solution.

There is also the issue of keeping the *Apple Mac OS X* version and the *Microsoft Windows* version identically and simultaneously updated. Although this guarantees the compatibility of sessions and makes it easier for professionals who have to move from one studio to the other, it also imposes some limitations: if one operating system offers interesting possibilities, *Avid*'s programmers often choose not to include them to avoid creating problems for users of the other operating system and introducing differences that might be difficult to manage.

Here we provide some tips that should help when troubleshoot-

- DAE error -9060 was encountered.

- Could not save a copy in ''mixage'' because out_of_range:
  Cmn_PolyVectorImpl::At.

- ''Bus error'' in thread ''MainThread'', at address 0x0

- Assertion in ''/Volumes/Development/ws.Pro-
  Tools_9.0.3/AlturaPorts/NewFileLibs/FileFormat/Mac-
  Build/../../FF/Audio/FF_AudioFile.cpp'', line 748

- starting location for iterator invalid (Searching File
  System For: Campagna ore 7.1.L.wav)

- ''Segmentation fault'' in thread ''MainThread'' at address
  0x0

- Assertion in ''/Volumes/Development/vb_devbranch-
  _boondock/AlturaPorts/NewFileLibs/ FileFormat/Mac-
  Build/../../BDM/BDM_TaskGroup.cpp'',line 28

- The engine DSP ran into the TDM2 deadband. Too many
  I/Os to the TDM2 chip. (-6074)

- Could not complete the Open Recent Session 2 command
  because An access violation has occurred. while
  translating Tracks.

- Can't import the selected video file because it does
  not have the same frame rate as the current video in
  the session. Video file frame rate is 4.119fps.

- Some regions were truncated or removed from the region
  list or timeline because they referred to files which
  are too short.

- Assertion in ''../../NewFileLibs/FF/Audio/Elastic-
  /FF_PacketIterator.h'', line 74

- The current playback engine does not support a sample
  rate of 0 kHz.

Table 8.1: A selection of Pro Tools spicy errors, hardly user friendly,
which I have encountered over the years.

ing typical instances of real or apparent malfunctions.

Let's say that the automatic upgrade of the operating system hosting Pro Tools is not advisable: normally *Avid* verifies and certifies compatibility several weeks after the upgrade has been made available to the public and often an update is necessary for Pro Tools to restore complete compatibility.

With regard to apparent malfunctioning it is interesting to note the variety of possible causes related to, for example, an *audio track* that will not play:

1. The amplifier is disconnected, muted, turned all the way down, gone into *safe-mode*, or even switched off.

2. The faders are at a very low level or the mixer module is muted.

3. A mixer module is in *solo* and therefore causing the other modules to be temporarily muted, including the one we want to hear or one of the *aux inputs* through which the signal is passing.

4. There is a *master fader* (maybe not shown) through which the signal should pass and its fader is lowered.

5. The assignment of physical outputs is wrong (in which case you should refer to the "I/O..." setting in the output page).

6. An *audio track* through which the signal should pass is set to *playback* instead of *input monitoring*, or it is not record/enabled.

7. The track does not have an assigned voice, is not activated, or the output is incorrect or inactive (use [COMMAND]+[CTRL]+click on the output selector).

8. The monitor system allows certain loudspeakers to be silenced and those that ought to be playing have been silenced.

9. The *clip* we want to playback is *offline* (its parent file hadn't been found and relinked) or silenced, perhaps by a very low *clip gain*.

10. There is a faulty cable or a problem with a connector, or a *patch bay* is faulty or a connector is inserted that is interrupting the *normalisation*.

11. You are not listening to the right audio interface or there's a *mute* on it.

"Real" problems arise mainly due to corrupted system support files or because of corrupted files related to a specific session. Since many of the files are automatically rebuilt if Pro Tools cannot find them it will often be enough to quit the app, remove them, reboot the system, be patient for a few minutes while the system verifies that everything is back to normal, and then manually restore the customisation of the preferences and settings.

Also verify if the drives (including the one containing the operating system) are in good condition or need repairing. With Mac OS X you should use the "Disk Utility" application, which is found in the "Utilities" subfolder of the "Applications" folder. We also suggest repairing the permissions in the start-up disc.

If the application does not launch, simply try being patient: in some cases, usually after a system crash, loading seems to be going nowhere but if you wait for five or so minutes it resumes and the problem is magically solved.

8.1   Problems in every session

Try removing several user-specific preferences. Files or folders that fall into this category are:

- the file "Pro Tools Prefs",

- the file "DigiSetup.OSX",

- the folder "DAE Prefs".

After quitting Pro Tools, by accessing the "Preferences" folder in the user's "Library" (on *OS X Lion* and *Mountain Lion* usually it's invisible but can be accessed with the "Go" option in the Finder menu while holding [OPTION]), remove them to the trash bin, switch off the computer and all peripheral units, then turn the peripheral devices back on and restart the computer.

Also try logging in to the operating system as another user. If the problem persists then remove the "Databases" folder, which can be accessed from the system "Library" (not the user "Library") under "/Application Support/Avid[1]/Pro Tools".

8.2 Problems in a specific session

Have you changed the names of folders or files used in the session, maybe when Pro Tools was running, or have you moved them? This could be the source of your troubles. Also remember that audio and video file names cannot contain certain characters, for instance the *slash* creates problems with video files. Also check that the names are not too long.

Without the need to quit Pro Tools, close the session and remove the "WaveCache.wfm" file that contains the waveform graphics. Providing you are using a version previous to 10, you can also remove the "Fades" folder/s (there could be more than one) related to the troublesome session. Then reload it.

Pro Tools performs automatic backups that you can retrieve from the dedicated folder "Session File Backups": start by opening one of the more recent of these backups.

If you cannot solve the problem then try removing the "Databases" folder, as described earlier, which will be rebuilt automatically when Pro Tools is next opened.

If there is still no improvement then create a new session with the same characteristics as the problematic session as far as file formats, sample frequency, and bit depth are concerned and then import all the tracks from the troublesome session.

Sometimes the problem lies in not being able to import some tracks in a new session. A way of circumventing this problem can be to create a *clip group*, export it and then import it to the new session. The *automation* can be recovered by removing the clips, leaving the automation, on the old session and then importing just the automation.

If you are still not successful try the *binary search*: import the first half of the tracks to determine if the problem lies there and, if not, import the second half. By continuing to divide by two you can

---

[1]"Digidesign" instead of "Avid" on less recent Pro Tools versions.

identify the problematic track, reverting it from a backup session made before the problem occurred.

8.3   Resources on the Web

For troubleshooting, and to keep updated about Pro Tools related news from *Avid Audio* and the countless partners that are involved in the development of additional *plug-ins*, the use of the *Web* is priceless. We mention here some sources where you can start:

- `http://duc.avid.com` is the immense *Avid Audio Forums*, where you can find user discussions, answers to the most frequently asked questions (*FAQ*), and news updates.

  At the bottom of the main page you can find links to additional resources, such as tutorial videos (there is also the link to a specific *YouTube* channel), and even special offers.

  The documentation in PDF format can be retrieved starting here: `http://www.avid.com/US/support`.

- In almost every nation there is at least one online group of Pro Tools fans discussing the software in their own language (for example, in Italy we have `http://www.protoolers.com`, founded by Andrea Caretti and Oliver Gambarini). A search of the *Web* should quickly reveal the best forums for you.

- `http://protools.ideascale.com` is the *Pro Tools Feedback Community*, where users suggest how *Avid Audio* could improve Pro Tools.

- `http://www.protoolerblog.com` with news, tips, reviews, contests and topics to discuss. It would be interesting to check the free RTAS plug-ins list.

- `http://www.pro-tools-expert.com` is a huge community for users for both music and post production, with over one million visits a year.

- `http://www.bluecataudio.com` offers some very interesting plug-ins for free.

- Try the marvellous Pro Tools User LinkedIn user group.

- Go for these video lessons: `http://play.macprovideo.com/library/app/ProTools`.

- Find some news about this book, and a list of free plug-ins, here: `http://www.gtcs.it/websitegtcs/English/Entries/2012/11/21_Pro_Tools_resources.html`, or contacting the author.

CHAPTER 9

Miscellaneous

9.1 Plug-in authorisation with iLok

Most of the software extensions for Pro Tools and (due to the removal of the limitation of using only *Avid*, *Digidesign*, and *M-audio* hardware) even Pro Tools itself from version 9, use a system against piracy requiring a USB device called *iLok* that is able to contain all the necessary licences, including those for the time-limited demo versions.

To use *iLok*, you have to create an account at http://www.iLok.com and then send the account details to the manufacturer of the *plug-in*, so that they can automatically place, provided that payment has been completed, a licence onto your account. You can manage one or more iLoks and transfer licences onto them. If not included during the Pro Tools installation, when you access the site you will be prompted to download and install the latest version of the necessary drivers.

You can take out an annual insurance called *Zero Downtime* that covers the *iLok*'s loss, theft, or damage. Should your *iLok* suffer from such an unlucky occurrence you would be rapidly supplied with a temporary version of the licence/s that you can, with no further cost and while waiting to receive a final version of such, deposit on a spare *iLok*.

9.2   An introduction to audio levels

Analogue Sound   In the analogue world, therefore mainly referring to recording on *magnetic tape* that was the successful protagonist of the technical scene for about half a century, the dynamic lower and upper limits were represented respectively by tape *hiss* and *saturation*, as in photography you have *grain* in case of underexposure and *burning* in the case of overexposure.

A *reference signal* was used, recorded at the head of the tape, which indicated a particular level that was not to be exceeded with continuous signals, and which represented 100% of the possible modulation. Rapid peaks that exceeded this level by no more than about 10 dB were tolerated because, due to the nature of tape saturation, they were barely perceptible.

The level indicator was a *VU-meter*, which, given its slowness[1] in registering the level to be measured, would perfectly mask the above mentioned peaks and was used to avoid crossing the 100% mark, i.e. the instrument's zero VU. The *reference signal* was, and still is, a 1,000 Hz sinusoidal tone.

Returning to our comparison with photography, we could identify the well-recognised *18% reflective grey* as being the equivalent of the audio reference signal. In photography that grey is placed about two *stops*[2] below the maximum level of brightness that the photochemical film can stand, outside which the tones become "bent", bouncing on a relatively smooth "ceiling", losing details; on average this supplies a good result when using the permitted dynamic range in analogue photography. Note that two *stops* is equivalent to 12 dB.

Digital vs Analogue   Digital sound, when in the common form of non-floating point *PCM*, has perceptual characteristics that are very different from analogue magnetic sound: when the signal is very low we have the *quantisation distortion*, a sort of crumpling of the sound on itself[3], while for strong signals the distortion lowers instead of

---

[1]About 300 ms is the perfect value to smooth the level's indication, so that you can read the value on the instrument when the signal is, for instance, spoken word

[2]A *stop* corresponds to a double/halving of the light.

[3]We can imagine the *quantisation distortion* as the deformation of a figure when the tesseras of a mosaic work that represent it are too few (for example 5x5 instead of 1000x1000).

increasing with the level, to then instantaneously and brutally become unacceptable as soon as you cross the 0 dB FS ceiling[4].

It turns out to be necessary to set an equivalence between the analogue and the digital reference levels. We have to consider that, as has been said, compared to that steady level you need usually about ten decibels more for rapid peaks and some further decibels as tolerance for human errors, not to mention the further *headroom* needed by the destructive audio encoding and decoding (*codec*) algorithms, such as *MP3*, *AAC*, and *Dolby AC-3*.

Therefore, a sinusoidal 1 kHz tone with peak equal to -18 dB FS has been defined by *EBU* and *ITU* as the *digital reference signal*, whereas a sinusoid with a -20 dB FS peak was choosed by *SMPTE* and adopted worldwide for cinema. Digital Reference

Nevertheless, the limitation on the *maximum permitted level* has slowly moved in some cases from the roughly 10 dB initially allowed to let us touch upon 0 dB FS, which means going up to a good 18 dB (20 dB for *SMPTE* and cinema) above the reference.
A very conservative peak-limit, which is valid in almost all cases but that limits the dynamics, is represented by 6 dB above the reference (this is valid even for the film's optical soundtrack), while the most used one in broadcast is 9 dB above the reference, using a *QPPM meter*.

Limiters and (also multiband) *compressors* are used to ensure that a mix respects such limits, or you can record at a lower level, which runs the very real risk of sticking out like a sore thumb when compared to other broadcast material and will probably require some output-level compensation (see figure 9.1, page 110). The *ATSC A/85* and the *EBU R-128* norms introduced important news starting from 2011 in relation to this: primarily, to promote mixes with a wider dynamic, normalisation should be to a target *loudness* value that is calculated as an average over the whole of the programme to be aired[5].

All of the above has to be integrated by introducing the concept of *acoustic alignment*, which is to say to set a precise scale factor Acoustic alignment

---

[4]The floating-point encoding is in truth changing things for the better. This brief introduction does not allow us to go into so much detail.

[5]I suggest reading the very clear and concise *ITU-R BS.1770 Revisited*, by Thomas Lund, available as a PDF on the Web.

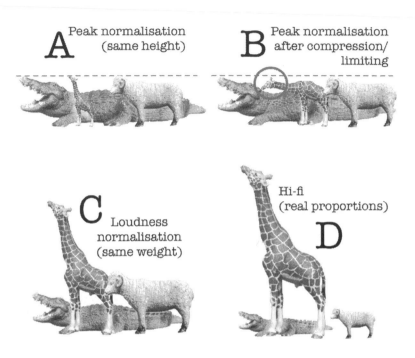

Figure 9.1: Normalisation of different audio sources, such as for music played on a radio show, which includes recordings from different times, places, and sound engineers.

Case A requires the listener's intervention on the fader that regulates the volume, case B (the most widespread presently) distorts the internal dynamic of each piece and flattens the differences, case C is usually better and can also be automated, case D is the ideal choice but requires high-quality listening systems. The use of related metadata could usefully shift the choice to the listener, who could then make a more informed decision on whether to use one of the four options (or perhaps a mix of two of them).

Thanks to my daughters for the toys!

between stimulus and effect, namely between the signal and the sound pressure it produces at the position where it is to be heard.

Cinema has defined long ago the following acoustic alignment: by feeding the front channels one at a time with a specific signal[6] you have to obtain 85 dB (this measurement has to be taken in C-weighting) of acoustic pressure at the optimal listening point. For the left and right surround channels you will have to obtain 82 dB. The *subwoofer* will have to be calibrated to guarantee an additional 10 dB of amplification when compared to the hypothetical response of the ideally perfect front loudspeakers.

In broadcasting, sound engineers tend to set these values a little lower. However, the recording industry is a jungle, and the well-known *loudness war* has brought about mixes with less and less dynamics[7].

After this short introduction the importance will be clear, in terms of quality, of properly centring our signals in respect of the transit channels, so that the sound goes through Pro Tools in an optimal way. In respect to this, let's consider the following also:

- Fixed-point *PCM* audio files cannot have samples that exceed 0 dB FS nominal (FS stands for *Full Scale* and 0 dB mathematically equals 100%). Potential problems are almost eliminated with 32-bit floating point files.

- *Plug-ins*, except the newest *AAX* type, have the same limits as the above mentioned fixed point audio files, both in the input and output stages.

  There is also the possibility that, although not clipping during input or output, some ill-designed plug-ins can cause clipping internally while performing the calculations that are necessary to generate the result.

- Pro Tools buses are very well sized and it is extremely difficult to reach their dynamic limits. We can therefore consider

---

[6]The test signal is an audio-band-limited *pink noise*, whose *RMS* level is equal to that of a 1,000 Hz sinusoid with a peak level of -20 dB FS.

[7]Bob Katz has done a very effective video entitled "Loudness War and Peace" on this subject, which you can see at http://www.digido.com/loudness-war-explained.html.

EQ III input
meter

them as almost representing no risk as far as clipping is concerned. But please notice, for example, that the *EQ III* input meter makes the measurement after the *input gain*, not indicating the clipping when a signal coming from a bus goes over 0 dB FS!

- Pro Tools faders allow the sound engineer's fingers to make precise adjustments, mainly around the 0 dB position, usually between -15 and +12 dB. Nevertheless, while the attenuation exponentially increases as the fader goes down, so that it is possible to reach any attenuation value, the possibility of going above +12 dB is inhibited. Therefore, according to the kind of sound material, it will be necessary to calibrate the mixer so that such maximum amplification will suffice for most of the time (in rare cases, we would use the equalisation gain, for example).

Because the *master faders* can attenuate the signal before delivering it to the *inserts*, we can apply some tricks to slightly increase our mixer's *headroom* or we have to keep the amplification of the listening system appropriately high to guarantee that the mixer works at levels that are sufficiently far from *clipping* at any stage[8].

---

[8]At http://www.gtcs.it an audio file for the calibration of the listening system is available, according to the *Gruppo Tematico per la Cinematografia Sonora* (Sonic Cinematography Thematic Group) standards, which suggests 8 dB of more *headroom* than cinema standard.

Short bio of the author

Simone Corelli is a film sound engineer (who also loves to play harpsichord). He was born in Milan, Italy at the end of 1969.

In 1997, after a degree in Information Sciences with a thesis on the correlation between musical perception and acoustics, he moved to Rome where a bizarre destiny carried him into the world of cinematographic sound.

He started out as an expert of Digidesign audio systems (he has been Pro Tools beta tester for five years); after an initial experience as a sound editor he decided to concentrate on mixing film soundtracks.

He concurrently teaches audio in Masters programmes at various universities, as well as in seminars at private institutions in Italy and Switzerland; he is also a frequent contributor to some technical magazines.

In 2006, together with Mr Felici and Mr Martinelli, he published the book *Elementi di Cinematografia Sonora*, with a foreword by Giuseppe Tornatore and an introduction by Professor Federico Savina.

He is member of the Italian *Audio Engineering Society*'s Advisory Board and of the *Associazione Italiana Fonici di Mix* (*AIFM*), and a co-founder of the *Gruppo Tematico per la Cinematografia Sonora* (*GTCS*).

Index

Made in the USA
Charleston, SC
28 January 2015